Love in the Pot

Walking in Truth

A Humble Chef's Culinary Guide

By
By Chana E. B. Israel

Copyright © 2023
All Rights Reserved

Contents

Dedication i
Acknowledgments ii
About the Author iii
Goals to Obtain 2
Apply & Achieve 3
Introduction 1
The Lord's High Holy Days 2
Sabbath Prep Tips 3
Keep the High Holy Days 5
Our Punishment 6
Our Duty 7
Change From the Inside Out 8
The Ten Commandments 9
No More Excuses 10
Terms & Acronyms 11
Let's Begin… 14
Chapter 1: Kitchen Organization 15
Chapter 2: Sanitation & Food Safety 27
Chapter 3: Cutting 101 32
Chapter 4: Methods 34
Chapter 5: What Kind of Cook Are You? 36
Chapter 6: Let's Cook 38
Chapter 7: Tips for Success 45
Chapter 8: Frying 48
Chapter 9: Nutrition 53
Chapter 10: Eat To Live and Eat Lawfully 55
Chapter 11: Prep for Success 60
Chapter 12: Recipes & More 63
Chapter 13: Unleavened Bread 164
References 195

Dedication

I'd like to dedicate this book to my loving husband. Without his encouragement, none of this would be possible! My hopes are to offer spiritually based culinary guidance to my children and to those women striving to walk in truth.

Acknowledgments

A special thanks to my family and congregation for all the love and support! Also, I'd like to give a shout out to all the amazing ladies that were able to review this project in its earlier stages. I appreciate the charity & time invested to offer feedback; y'all rock!

About the Author

Examine yourselves, whether ye be in the faith; prove your own selves. Know ye not your own selves, how that Jesus Christ is in you, except ye be reprobates?
2 Corinthians 13:5

I'm Chana: wife, mother of 4 & culinary artist. I've been happily married to an amazing man for over 18 years! All while growing the bond of marriage & raising children, I've been able to blossom in cooking. To this day, culinary arts is a huge part of my life. Even as I walk in truth, the art of cooking remains a key element in my routine. Here's my story; an entanglement of cooking, love & repentance.

My current state of reflection & "self-examination".

How did my culinary journey begin? How did I begin to walk in truth? How am I becoming the "new me"?

Since the very beginning, before I even knew better, I've been drawn to cooking. Creating is my passion! My mother has a collection of stories to tell of my relationship with cooking. Once, she awoke from a nap to a smoky house! Mom ran, following the trail of smoke. Low & behold, it was 7-year-old me wondering what the matter was. "What are you doing child?", she demanded. I sweetly said, "I'm making collard dreens (collard greens) & panny cakes" (corn cakes). It's funny to look back on now! Thank God that I didn't get injured or burn the house down!

From that day on, my mom knew that she needed to teach me how to safely cook. She got me a little kitchenet toy to boot, lol! It's amazing how gracious God has been to me! He's been protecting me for so long, even in my oblivion.

Throughout my childhood, somehow, the Lord has always led me into a kitchen. I remember many occasions of making hard caramel candies or peanut brittle for the family. Or, making cupcakes to sell with my childhood buddy during the summers for "fun" money. I may have only been about 11 years old. Eventually, I became the household cook. So, you see, this must be exactly what God intends for me. The kitchen has been my landing zone for most of my life. I'd like to believe that in using my culinary gifts, I am serving God & helping others with it.

Years later, I graduated with honors & earned a degree in culinary arts. I've had the opportunity to work several areas in the field. Because of this, I've been blessed to attain much knowledge along the way. Here's my advice to those determined cooks...

Flexibility is the name of the game for most developing chefs. Thus, you are able to work in a variety of capacities to earn income & gain experience. This was certainly the case for me. Afterall, desired positions are difficult to obtain. No one wants to hire the inexperienced. So, see it as an opportunity for growth, not as a downside!

Today, I'm a homemaker, homeschooler of 4 & retired from the traditional work force. This allows me to focus efforts on my family, helping my church & using my talent to do the Lord's work – planning & cooking.

Now, I strive daily to renew myself. To walk in truth means to change & live according to the dos & don'ts of the Bible. It is an ongoing process that requires devotion, studying & patience. This even translates to reforming from the kitchen (what you prepare & consume) to within (spiritual cleansing). I endeavor daily to reform my life to align with the scriptures & my husband's needs.

Back to cooking… Presently, I'm working on our terms as a personal chef. You can even find me demonstrating culinary tips on my YouTube channel titled "Love In The Pot". Note: I am no "techie"! Lord willing, my editing will get better.

Influence selflessly… Cooking may not always be fun, but it certainly affects many. It is a selfless commitment that we must all find a way to enjoy. Afterall, we have an amazing ability & a power within us! We can help foster & maintain good health through delicious food preparations. Be proud & find your love within the kitchen.

The unspoken reality… Like all things, there are two perspectives to every story. I'd like to mention to those aspiring chefs, this is no easy field! You could become successful with time, patience & experience. Loving the craft is a must! A viable career in the cooking industry will require lots of hard work & sacrifice.

Chef's Perspective

The kitchen has become my home, even though I've tried to avoid it. However, you should not take it lightly when considering this as a career. Striving for a suitable income earning position in the culinary world should be well thought out.

Realistically speaking… culinary work is tough! It puts lots of wear and tear on the feet, back, neck, hands, & even the ability to get a full night's sleep. Not to mention that it is highly stressful & demanding. Its demands will not only affect you but will also impact family time.

Someone always wants something to eat! That warm bakery bread or those freshly baked donuts took time & care. A baker or pastry professional likely worked from midnight to the morning to have them ready for your convenience. This is certainly not the field to choose just for fun. You must love it! *I'm finally embracing that it's my destiny & love it; I do!*

I have even had the honor of serving & cooking for those of my church. To maintain balance; prayer, planning & check lists make it all possible.

My hopes are to help the average or novice cook. I'd like to demonstrate a less overwhelming way to prep & expand your culinary skills. Making more on your own will have several positive results. You will be more empowered to eat less defiled foods & gain more nutritional awareness! Not to mention that you will be enabled to ensure that your meals are kosher.

Cook With Passion

Why is it said, "We must cook with passion"? Well… Cooking is an act of love. It is one of the ultimate ways to offer charity. In its purest form, it is alms. Cooking takes patience, thoughtfulness & hard work. Meal preparation is an expression of nurturing & care. It is one of the most important ways to show someone that you love them.

What joy it brings to know that the love was received & appreciated! Especially if it was healthy, kosher & delicious! A hug in a dish… So, suit up; let's get to the meat of this book & begin the journey of "walking in truth"!

For alms doth deliver from death, and shall purge away all sin. Those that exercise alms and righteousness shall be filled with life.
Tobit 12:9

Then he said unto them, Go your way, eat the fat, and drink the sweet, and send portions unto them for whom nothing is prepared: for this day is holy unto our Lord: neither be ye sorry; for the joy of the Lord is your strength.
Nehemiah 8:10

"Who can find a virtuous woman? For her price is far above rubies." Proverbs 31:10

"She seeketh wool, and flax, and worketh willingly with her hands." Proverbs 31:13

Goals to Obtain

- **Kitchen Basics**: Gain new skills & learn to make your kitchen work for you.
- **Reformation From The Kitchen To Within**: Learn to cook with love! Grasp the concept of biblically-based kosher cooking. Explore how to make the Lord's High Holy Days special in your household.
- **Walking In Truth**: Learn how to eat according to the biblical dietary laws and guide your house around God's laws, statutes, and commandments.
- **Let's Get Cooking**: Apply the techniques taught to make delicious recipes and learn to personalize them to suit you and your family's needs.

Apply & Achieve

If you apply the right techniques, tools, and methods, you can make nearly anything!

Anyone can cook the basics. But, if you expand your abilities & increase your "culinary superpowers", you'll be able to offer more variations & nutrition to your loved ones. Not only is this more affordable, but it will certainly be more fun! Apply this interactive cooking ability while having your family's health & spirit in mind.

Join me on this journey to walking in truth.
For we are his workmanship, created in Christ Jesus unto good works, which God hath before ordained that we should walk in them.
Ephesians 2:10

Introduction

She looketh well to the ways of her household, and eateth not the bread of idleness
Proverbs 31:27

Self-examination. Awareness. Fusion: all three of these terms come to mind as I reflect on life today. My career stamps me as a chef, but I am also a follower of Christ. Yes, this can pose many conflicts in life! It is very difficult to be in the world but not of it… But, I am a walking example that a Bible-based life is possible. Here's a little insight into how I began to walk in truth & apply the Bible from the kitchen to within.

My journey to repentance began with three initial goals: to be a good wife, to support & maintain the good health of my family, and to guide my children accordingly to God's requirements. I am still a work in progress…

Many women are striving to take on the characteristics of the positive foremothers of the Bible. Such women aim to follow the righteous examples mentioned in Proverbs chapter 31 & Titus chapter 2.

A huge part of that spiritual nurturing involves building your household on a strong foundation- a foundation based on God's laws, statutes & commandments. This source of strength should influence us, women, to go above & beyond! It is our duty to make God & our husbands proud! All good practices should begin at home & display charity through love.

A repenting woman understands that this foundation is significant in spiritual growth; what better way to show such commitment than through joyful spiritual cooking!

Feeding our families a well-balanced, nutritious diet is something we all should learn to enjoy! It is a beautiful thing to know that you've fed your loved ones with the best options available to you. This is always what I aim to do. Yes, this all can be done while meeting the dietary requirements of the Bible. Of course, the occasional pizza or special treat is not denied…

Just know that the concept of making most things from scratch can be done! This will not require breaking the bank. Home-cooked meals may not always be conducive. But, as much as possible, you should strive to do so. Hopefully, this little guidebook can offer some helpful kitchen tips, advice & spiritual inspiration.

Beloved, I wish above all things that thou mayest prosper and be in health, even as thy soul prospereth. 3 John 1:2

The Lord's High Holy Days

- Keep the Sabbaths (Friday Sundown to Saturday sundown, Leviticus 23:32)
- Keep the New Moons, beginning of months (every full moon, Ecclesiasticus 43:6-8)
- Passover (The Feast of Unleavened Bread)
- The Day of Simon
- Feast of First Fruits (Pentecost)
- Memorial of Blowing of Trumpets
- Day of Atonement (the fast to atone for sins- eat nothing, Leviticus 23:27)
- Feast of Tabernacles
- Feast of Dedication (also known as Hanukkah)
- Destruction of Nicanor
- Purim

Beautify your home, decorate, cook a special meal, and make a big deal on the Lord's High Holy Days!

"This is the day which the Lord hath made; we will rejoice and be glad in it."
Psalm 118:24

Sabbath Prep Tips

Did you know that the Bible is full of holidays? These are referred to as "High Holy Days". We are to celebrate the appointed holidays of the Bible, not of the world. The Lord has given us many High Holy Days to enjoy! More than you would imagine.

The most frequent High Holy Day is the Sabbath, of course! With that said, I'd like to share a few tips for preparation. These things have eased my workload. Hopefully, they can help you too!

Tips To Simplify Sabbath Prep:

- *Plan Ahead*: Plan your intended meals & shop for the ingredients earlier in the week. Wednesday may be a good day to do so. By the way, you can also shop online & save time!

- *Divide & Conquer*: Split up the prep. You could create baked goods & cook breakfast meats on Thursday. Then, finalize the Sabbath meal prep on Friday (cut the fresh fruit & make sandwiches/ a side salad).

- *Have Dinner In Place*: Create an oven ready dinner option ahead of time. It will make all the difference! You can assemble & freeze an easy casserole dish on Monday that can be baked prior to sundown Friday. Or, you can simply order & pay for takeout prior to sundown.

- *Make It Semi-Homemade*: Combine homemade items with quality store bought products to save time. Trim your prep by buying pre-made composed salads to accompany your sandwiches (taste & adjust it if necessary). You could even purchase bakery fresh muffins, pastries and pre-cut fresh fruit to reduce the workload. Don't forget to check product labels & ensure that the ingredients are clean (without pork, shellfish or any unlawful products)!

REMEMBER…

NO FIRE TO COOK – FROM FRIDAY SUNDOWN TO SATURDAY SUNDOWN

Ye shall kindle no fire throughout your habitations upon the sabbath day.
Exodus 35:3

PREP AHEAD - BEFORE SUNDOWN FRIDAY

(the Sabbath begins at sundown Friday & ends at sundown Saturday)

And he said unto them, This is that which the LORD hath said, Tomorrow is the rest of the holy sabbath unto the LORD: bake that which ye will bake today, and seethe that ye will seethe; and that which remaineth over lay up for you to be kept until the morning.
Exodus 16:23

HONOR THE SABBATH DAY

Remember the sabbath day, to keep it holy.
Exodus 20:8

CONGREGATE ON THE SABBATH DAY

Not forsaking the assembling of ourselves together, as the manner of some is; but exhorting one another: and so much the more, as ye see the day approaching.
Hebrews 10:25

Keep the High Holy Days

Prepare an amazing feast, joyfully congregate and make it Holy!

"(3) Blow up the trumpet in the new moon, in the time appointed, on our solemn feast day. (4) For this was a statue for Israel, and a law of the God of Jacob."
Psalms 81:3-4

"And thine ears shall hear a word behind thee, saying, This is the way, walk ye in it, when ye turn to the right hand, and when ye turn to the left."
Isaiah 30:21

"(37) These are the feasts of the Lord, which ye shall proclaim to be holy convocations, to offer an offering made by fire unto the Lord, a burnt offering, and a meat offering, a sacrifice, and drink offerings, everything upon his day: (38) Beside the sabbaths of the Lord, and beside your gifts, and beside all your vows, and beside all your freewill offerings, which ye give unto the Lord."
Leviticus 23:37-38

"Serve the Lord with gladness: come before his presence with singing."
Psalms 100:2

Our Punishment

To this day, we are experiencing suffering in some form for not upholding God's laws. Let's work to reverse our punishment & gain entrance to the kingdom of heaven! We must endure.

"Behold, we are yet this day in our captivity, where thou hast scattered us, for a reproach and a curse, and to be subject to payments, according to all the iniquities of our fathers, which departed from the Lord our God."
Baruch 3:8

"(47) Because thou servedst not the Lord thy God with joyfulness, and with gladness of heart, for the abundance of all things; (48) Therefore shalt thou serve thine enemies which the Lord shall send against thee, in hunger, and in thirst, and in nakedness, and in want of all things: and he shall put a yoke of iron upon thy neck, until he have destroyed thee."
Deuteronomy 28:47-48

"For whatsoever things were written aforetime were written for our learning, that we through patience and comfort of the scriptures might have hope."
Romans 15:4

The Bible is written in masculine form. However, God's words pertain to both men & women. We must confess our faults, repent & keep God's laws, statutes, and commandments!

Our Duty

1. To Repent

"Repent ye therefore, and be converted, that your sins may be blotted out, when the times of refreshing shall come from the presence of the Lord;" Acts 3:19

2. To Apply the Bible & Change

Changing our behavior to meet God's standards is our "reasonable service and sacrifice".

"(1) I beseech you therefore, brethren, by the mercies of God, that ye present your bodies a living sacrifice, holy, acceptable unto God, which is your reasonable service. (2) And be not conformed to this world: but be ye transformed by the renewing of your mind, that ye may prove what is that good, and acceptable, and perfect, will of God."
Romans: 12:1-2

"She is like the merchants' ships; she bringeth her food from afar." Proverbs 31:14
"(26) She openeth her mouth with wisdom; and in her tongue is the law of kindness. (27) She looketh well to the ways of her household, and eateth not the bread of idleness." Proverbs 31:26-27

3. To Fear God and Keep His Commandments

"Let us hear the conclusion of the whole matter: Fear God, and keep his commandments: for this is the whole duty of man." Ecclesiastes 12:13

"And he said to them all, If any man will come after me, let him deny himself, and take up his cross daily, and follow me." Luke 9:23

"That ye might walk worthy of the Lord unto all pleasing, being fruitful in every good work, and increasing in the knowledge of God;" Colossians 1:10

Change From the Inside Out

You can do this! Strive to live righteously according to God's standards. Repent, study (2 Timothy 2:15), and apply the laws, statutes, and commandments daily. Aim to convert your spirit as you are converting your kitchen. Eat clean & live righteously. It starts from within!

"For a just man falleth seven times, and riseth up again: but the wicked shall fall into mischief." Proverbs 24:16

"(47) Yet if they shall bethink themselves in the land whither they were carried captives, and repent, and make supplication unto thee in the land of them that carried them captives, saying, We have sinned, and have done perversely, we have committed wickedness; (48) And so return unto thee with all their heart, and with all their soul, in the land of their enemies, which led them away captive, and pray unto thee toward their land, which thou gavest unto their fathers, the city which thou hast chosen, and the house which I have built for thy name: (49) Then hear thou their prayer and their supplication in heaven thy dwelling place, and maintain their cause," 1 Kings 8:47-49

"Wherefore the law is holy, and the commandment holy, and just, and good." Romans 7: 12

"For this is the love of God, that we keep his commandments: and his commandments are not grievous." 1 John 5:3

God's Word Is Truth – Do As Instructed
"Sanctify them through thy truth: thy word is truth." John 17:17

"(16) All scripture is given by inspiration of God, and is profitable for doctrine, for reproofs, for correction, for instruction in righteousness: (17) That the man of God may be perfect, throughly furnished unto all good works." 2 Timothy 3:16-17

The Ten Commandments

Read it in its entirety.

"(3) Thou shalt have no other gods before Me.

(4-5) Thou shalt not make unto thee any graven image or worship them.

(7) Thou shalt not take the name of the Lord thy God in vain

(8-11) Remember the sabbath day, to keep it holy.

(12) Honor thy father and thy mother

(13) Thou shalt not kill.

(14) Thou shalt not commit adultery.

(15) Thou shalt not steal.

(16) Thou shalt not bear false witness against thy neighbor (no lying)

(17) Thou shalt not covet ..." Exodus 20:1-17

No More Excuses

"Whatsoever thy hand findeth to do, do it with thy might; for there is no work, nor device, nor knowledge, nor wisdom, in the grave, whither thou goest." Ecclesiastes 9:10

Make It Happen…

Despite our busy lives, we must not neglect to feed our families healthy meals. Simply put, we must eat the rainbow. Colorful foods offer different nutritional values and are available in a variety of fresh fruits & vegetables.

To my advantage, I happen to be a chef. Don't worry; with a little kitchen organization, a few culinary basics, and an open mind, you too can incorporate a more balanced diet.

I'd like to share a few professional tips & culinary concepts. From a chef's standpoint, cooking is all about passion, method & technique. The question is: which method to use to achieve the desired result. If you apply the correct method & technique; with practice, you can make nearly anything.

Let's get started with the basics; kitchen 101.

Terms & Acronyms

To understand some of the terms & acronyms used, the vocabulary has been added to the beginning of this book.

Basic Culinary Terms:

- **EVOO**: Extra Virgin Olive Oil.
- **TT**: To taste
- **S & P**: Salt and Pepper.
- **V.X.**: Vanilla Extract.
- **I.Q.F. (individually quick frozen):** to freeze individual food pieces or portions quickly & in a loose single layer; ensuring that the pieces aren't touching
- **Chef's Knife**: All-purpose knife used for chopping, slicing, and mincing (8-14" long blade which is wide at the heel and tapers to a point at the tip.
- **Tang**: A portion of the chef's knife blade that runs through the length of the handle.
- **Carryover Cooking:** The cooking that occurs after food is removed from a heat source due to residual heat that remains in the food.
- **Colander:** a perforated bowl used to strain off liquid from food
- **Baste**: To moisten foods during cooking (usually while grilling, broiling, or roasting) with melted fat, pan drippings, a sauce, or flavorful liquid to prevent drying and/or to add flavor.
- **Paring Knife:** A short knife used for detail work, carved designs or cutting fruits and vegetables
- **Mince:** To cut food into small, uniform pieces.
- **Chop**: To cut an item into small pieces where uniformity of size & shape isn't necessary.
- **Juilienne**: One of the 3 stick cuts in which food is cut into long, thin strips (1/8" x 1/8"x 2"). There are 3 French based stick cuts all increasing in size from thinnest to thickest (allumette- a matchstick or fine julienne cut, juilienne & batonette or fry cut.
- **Micro-plane:** A fine grater used to achieve a fine mince (great for hard cheeses, zest, or garlic)
- **Chiffonade (little ribbons)**: To finely slice or shred leafy vegetables or herbs.
- **Dice**: Cubed cuts formed into small, medium or large sizes

- **Blanch & Shock**: Very briefly and partially cooking food in boiling water followed by an immediate shock into an ice water bath which stops the cooking process.
- **Savory**: Describes spiced or seasoned foods as opposed to sweet.
- **Mise en place**: French for "putting in place" refers to the preparation & assembly of all necessary ingredients & equipment.
- **Mirepoix**: A mixture of 50% onions, 25% carrots, and 25% celery used as a flavor base for soups, sauces, and other dishes. **The Holy Trinity**: A Cajun version of the classic French mirepoix. This aromatic blend is an essential base in both Creole & Cajun cuisine. The mixture is a ratio of one part onion, one part celery & one part green bell pepper.
- **Nappe**: refers to sauce consistency, which should coat the back of a spoon.
- **Sauté:** A quick-cooking method with dry heat, using a hot pan and a small amount of fat.
- **Roasting:** A dry air/ dry heat method that is usually done in the oven or on open fire.
- **Render**: To melt and clarify fat; to cook meats to remove fat.
- **Sear**: To brown food quickly over high heat.
- **Roux**: Equal parts flour and fat, by weight; used as a thickener for sauces and other dishes
- **Rondelles or Rounds**: Easily made disk-shaped slices of cylindrical vegetables or fruits.
- **FIFO** (first in, first out); this systematic method of rotation is used in the culinary field to manage the proper rotation of foods during stocking. This helps to avoid spoilage & reduce waste in stores & food establishments. Thus, the same principle should be applied in home kitchens (ex: before opening a new jar of mayo, finish the one that's already open or use the item with the date closest to expiration first).
- **HACCP** (hazard analysis critical control points): A rigorous system of self-inspection used to manage & maintain sanitary conditions in all types of foodservice operations.
- **Mother Sauces:** The 5 French-based sauces that all sauces stem from (béchamel- cream, velouté- thickened chicken stock, Espagnole- brown sauce, tomato & hollandaise).
- **Legumes**: A large group of vegetables with double-seamed seed pods.
- **Leavener**: An ingredient or process that produces or incorporates gases in a baked product to increase volume (make rise), provide structure, and give texture.
- **Leavening Agents**: Manipulative leaveners- air, steam, carbon dioxide; (common kitchen leaveners- baking powder, baking soda, yeast & baking ammonia).

- **Thickening Agents**:

1) *Roux:* Equal parts flour & fat cooked together (3 types- white, blonde & brown: the darker its cooked, the deeper the flavor, resulting in lessened thickening power).

2) Cornstarch: Starch made from maize (corn) using the endosperm of the kernel.

3) *Slurry: A* mix of starch or flour and liquid combined until smooth.

4) *Arrowroot:* From roots of tropical plants.

5) *Beurre Manie:* A smooth flour and butter paste.

6) *Liaison:* Egg yolks and cream.

7) Coulis: A sauce made from a purée of vegetables and/or fruit (typically served on its own, hot or cold).

Let's Begin…

An organized kitchen incites inspiration, motivation, and excitement! Just looking at this picture makes me want to revamp my pantry too!

Get Organized: *Prep and Cook for Success!*

Shown above is a 5x3 personal chef meal service created by me! What is a personal chef service? This service usually offers a week of gourmet meals. These meals are custom, prepared ahead, and conveniently ready to heat. One example is the 5x3 meal plan. It represents 5 entrée meals per week to serve 3 people. This offers 15 entrée portions in total. How fantastic it would be to have such a service! A personal chef like myself would plan your meals ahead. Then, that chef would shop, cook, cool, leave instructions, label the meals & even clean your kitchen afterwards!

Chapter 1: Kitchen Organization

Kitchen 101:

The key to efficient and easy cooking is a kitchen organized around your personal needs.

- Recognize your cooking style.
- Arrange equipment around your needs and usage.
- Remember to label.
- Make it accessible.

What cooking methods do you typically use? If you make most of your meals on the stovetop, then sautéing is your usual cooking method. You may want to store sauté pans near the stovetop or even on a hanging pot rack. An assortment of oils labeled in squirt bottles near the range is ideal (examples: extra virgin olive oil, canola oil, avocado oil, clarified butter, etc.). Keeping small, labeled containers of spices used regularly is quite helpful (like salt, pepper, and garlic powder). This could be kept near the stove for quick and easy seasoning.

Storage

Store for accessibility. Your kitchen equipment should be stored in a way that allows for quick access to the items you use most. The things that are rarely used should occupy the least convenient space. Don't waste valuable counter space storing bulky equipment! Put those items away in the more inconvenient cabinets and storage places.

Utilize counter space with items needed regularly: A tool caddy, vessels holding spoons, rubber spatulas, and the bulky pieces you use most (coffee brewer, blender, etc.). Now, you will have more functioning work surfaces for food preparation. A magnetic wall-mounted knife holder is a great space saver too!

In my kitchen, I have large slender containers holding all the essential tools I use regularly. One holds wooden spoons/ spatulas, and another contains whisks. My vital gadgets (thermometers, garlic press, etc.) are all in one storage vessel. While a tool caddy safely holds all my knives and sharp items like the micro-plane, kitchen shears, and pizza cutter. These containers are all stored in my preferred prep space, which is near the stovetop for convenience.

Most importantly, remember cleanliness and sanitation! Cross-contamination is the easiest way to spread harmful bacteria throughout your kitchen and home. It's a great idea to have a motion censored soap dispenser for the kitchen and nearby access to paper towels. This helps prevent contaminating the soap pump and faucet. Turn on the faucet with your forearms, not your soiled hands. Then, turn off the faucet with a paper towel when done.

Eat Fresh When Possible

Potted herbs are a great addition! They add beauty, freshness, and additional nutrients to your meals. I absolutely love using fresh herbs and veggies from my little garden. The hard work and effort it takes to yield such fruits are evident. Homegrown foods taste so much better and sweeter than items bought in stores! They tend to last longer too.

Growing organic & nurturing my home garden translates to helping my husband! You, too, could start a small potted garden to reap these benefits. Most herbs, peppers, squash, peas, and green beans are easy to grow. Get started today. You can do this! Digital instructions and information are readily available with the press of a button.

Just keep in mind that it must be checked daily, watered when needed, pruned frequently, and fertilized regularly (weekly to bi-weekly). Search the web and gardening books, and even ask questions of the experts at local gardening centers to troubleshoot. YouTube can also be a helpful resource for "how tos" & to search for problem solving techniques.

My Home Garden - Grow More & Save – (If I can do it, so can you!)

Dark Leafy Greens & More

A day's pick (below)

Organic Golden Jubilee Tomatoes

Flowers & Blackberries

Herbs & Baby Plants (dino kale, tomatoes, beets & citronella)

Blueberries

Young Collards & Young Pepper Plants

Strawberries

Young Collards – Side View

Kale

Garden to table- radishes & colorful beets used to create a roasted veggie medley

Brown Turkey Fig

Chapter 2: Sanitation & Food Safety

- *Cross-contamination*: The transfer of bacteria or other contaminants from one food, work surface, or piece of equipment to another.
- *Clean*: To remove visible dirt and particles.
- *Sanitize*: To reduce pathogenic organisms to safe levels.

Impeccable sanitation is extremely important: A kitchen could be a potential danger zone. Not only are there hot surfaces and sharp objects, but there is always the risk of creating a germ-festering zone! Avoid the spread of germs or cross-contamination between tools, equipment, surfaces, and/or different foods.

Don't confuse cleaned with sanitized: A good rule of thumb is to clean and sanitize as you go. Here's how to clean thoroughly:

1. Wash: Always begin with properly washed hands. Follow this by washing the work surfaces. Then continue as mentioned below as needed and in between tasks.

- Rinse
- Sanitize

You should thoroughly wash with warm soapy water. Then rinse with clean, warm water. Now, sanitize counters & surfaces using Clorox or Lysol wipes. Or make up a bottle of sanitizing solution. Do this by using a spray bottle, clean water & bleach, or a disinfecting chemical made for kitchen use (follow dilution instructions on the chosen chemical bottle).

2. Form good kitchen habits: Before you begin cooking, make it a habit to clean and sanitize the kitchen surfaces, sink, and stove. Make life easy by using disinfecting wipes between tasks on the surfaces. As always, wash your hands before starting, as needed & any time prior to a new task. **You should know that maintaining good personal hygiene is extremely important.** Bacteria can also be transferred from your skin, hair, underneath the nails or even your clothing. So, be mindful to continue the practice of good personal hygiene. *In short: clean skin, clean clothes, clean surfaces and clean foods result in minimal contamination!*

3. Avoid cross-contamination! For example, after cutting and seasoning salmon, transfer the fish to a pan. Then put the dirty board and knife in the sink. You could simply deal with the veggies before working with the fish. However, you should properly wash the knife and board with antibacterial soap before reuse.

To simplify, I often use color-coded cutting boards. Here's a color code suggestion: use red for meat, orange for raw chicken, green for savory produce, yellow for fruits or sweet items like chocolate, and white for fish. This may seem tedious, but what you may not know is that boards can hold bacteria in the cut grooves. They can even retain certain tastes. So, I like to use separate boards to prevent cross-contamination or eating strawberries that taste like garlic, lol. By the way, stores offer thin color-coded varieties of plastic cutting boards. This will make storage much more convenient. However, these aren't my favorite option as they don't always lie flat and can often slip.

4. Always wash your hands before cooking and after handling any raw meat or fish! Never handle two types of meat without washing your hands and items used in between. Most meats have different temperatures of doneness. Remember to sanitize as you go (disinfectant wipes make things easier).

All raw meat, poultry, and fish have microscopic bacteria that can only be killed with proper heat exposure. They must be cooked to the correct internal temperature of doneness. Whenever handling or fabricating raw meat, poultry, eggs or fish, always, always, always wash your hands! You should also wash utensils used as well as sanitize your prep area when done.

5. Again, clean as you go! Wash your hands, and clean/ sanitize work surfaces between tasks. Never work with ready-to-eat items like salad or even prep veggies in an uncleaned area after dealing with raw meats. Don't get overwhelmed. Once your kitchen is organized and has the basic cooking supplies, this will all be easy.

Internal Cooking Temperatures for Doneness:
- Beef and lamb: 155° F
- Poultry: 165 ° F
- Fish: 145° F
- Eggs: 145° F, Egg Dishes- 160° F
- Stuffed Meats, Filled Pasta/ Casserole Dishes and Whole Poultry: 185° F

6. Handwashing: Proper handwashing is one of the most effective ways to prevent cross-contamination. Use warm water (as hot as you can stand), wet your hands, lather with soap, and wash for 20 or more seconds. During this scrub, you should thoroughly wash your palms, between fingers, under nails (use a brush or simply agitate the nails with soap in the palm—scratch soapy palm), on top of hands and wrists. Rinse well and use a paper towel to turn off the faucet if previously touched by dirty hands. I usually turn the water on with my forearm. Remember to constantly think of your hands as possible germ transmitters. Keep your hands as clean as possible!

Short nails are highly recommended: Did you know that bacteria could harbor under your fingernails? Just the thought of feces, dead dirty skin particles, and meat bacteria like salmonella resting deep under the nail is more than enough reasons to maintain noticeably short and clean nails.

Here are a few other key factors to master...

Time-Temperature Abuse:

This may be something the home cook has never heard of. Yet, it is one of the most important factors in the culinary field. Time-temperature abuse refers to exposing food to temperatures in which harmful bacteria can grow rapidly and potentially make food unsafe. A good rule of thumb is to keep cold foods cold & hot foods hot. Always try to avoid foods lingering in temperature on either end.

Why is this so important? When food is exposed to unsafe temperatures, food-borne illnesses could occur. Bacteria multiply rapidly in the range of temperatures between 41°F and 135°F. This is known as the temperature danger zone. Keep your food safe & help avoid spoilage by reducing these possibilities.

Proper Cooling:

To begin the cooling process, you should aim to cool hot food down to 70°F (about room temp.) within the first 2 hours. After this period, you have a total of 4 hours to get your dish cooled down to 41°F or below. Foods should not be exposed to the danger zone for more than a 6-hour period. This is extremely important to those who may have to prepare large quantities of food. This could also be a great risk for those with compromised immune systems – the elderly, young children or even pregnant women. It's a great idea to have several hotel pans or full-sized foil steam table pans available to use for this purpose (cooling). Just simply wash them for another day after you've completed the cooling process.

Cool Quickly: Here are some tips to assist with rapid cooling

- *Reduce the thickness!* A thinner layer of food will cool much faster (about 2-4 inches in depth). Use a few full-sized foil pans to get the job done.

- *Use an ice bath!* Using a foil pan filled with ice water may do the trick. Just add the pan of hot food on top of the icy water & stir often. Repeat this process until the dish reaches 70°F. You could also invest in a cooling paddle or simply use several new large frozen ice packs to mimic it. If a large ice pack is used, be sure to completely remove all labels. Or, put it in a clean, large zip bag to eliminate the chance of a physical contaminant. Note: An ice water bath is a great cooling technique for casserole dishes that can't be stirred. Just know that likely, the ice bath will need to be refreshed with new cold water & ice more often until the dish has cooled.

- *Stir Frequently!* Frequent stirring results in the use of friction to incorporate air. This will help to drop the temperature at a faster rate.

- *Refrigerate & Cover with Airflow!* Once the hot dish has reached a temperature of 70°F, cover it tightly with plastic wrap or foil & poke holes all around; refrigerate. This will help the food to continue to chill quickly. Once it is cold, cover the dish with an appropriate airtight lid or a new piece of foil.

Food Storage & Reheating:

To preserve the freshness & longevity of the prepared dish, it is recommended to store food in airtight food storage containers or bags. Whichever is best suited for the job, utilize your newly learned food safety skills on make ahead meals. I love preparing my F.O.T. meals ahead & freezing them for reheat. Now, you, too, could do so with food safety in mind.

When reheating food, you should heat it to an internal temperature of 165°F. Thus, increasing the chances of killing any harmful bacteria that may have grown during the cooling process. This can be ensured easily with the right tool. I highly suggest that you invest in a good quality digital food thermometer, a must-have in my kitchen. This handy tool can also be used to ensure that you cook your meats to the correct temperature of doneness. Cook with confidence & reduce undercooked or even dry overcooked meats.

Keep Food Safety At The Forefront!

Chef "O.", my former catering instructor, would say, "A chef must constantly be concerned with food safety. We must always think: Did I get anyone sick today?" With that said, you must wonder: Did that diarrhea come from a stomach bug, or was it simply a mild form of food poisoning? Never let your food safety guard down, Chef's rule!

Remember, this is a form of maintaining God's temple (your body). In doing so, this will provide another level of care for yourself as well as those nurtured in love with your food. This extra effort is definitely a form of brotherly love. So, help to avoid food-borne illnesses in your household!

"(6) And he hath given men skill, that he might be honoured in his marvellous works. (7) With such doth he heal men, and taketh away their pains."

Ecclesiasticus 38:6-7

Chapter 3: Cutting 101

The Chef's Knife (Most Used Tool):

Now that you have a great idea of how to set up your kitchen, here are some necessary culinary basics. There are a few things that every cook needs. Number one on my list is a great Chef's knife! I prefer one that has a tang that runs inside the entire handle of the knife. This makes for excellent support, durability, and balance.

Many amateur cooks are intimidated by the chef's knife. Honestly, once you know how to use it and become more comfortable with it, there will be no substitute. To be in control of this large knife, it must be held correctly. Hold the handle with three fingers while gripping the blade between the thumb and the index finger. I prefer a medium-weighted stainless-steel chef's knife. This blade is also a great beginner's option.

Let's Chop:

Now let's begin cutting. If you're right-handed, hold the handle as described above with that hand. The opposite hand is used to feed the food into the knife. The knife holding hand should be stationary. Slightly rock the knife up and down to achieve cutting. You should try not to glide the knife towards the food. Though, many of us do. As the item is cut, aim to gradually feed it towards the blade.

Always create a claw grip while handling the food item to be sliced:

This will greatly minimize any opportunity for accidental finger cuts. A correct hand position will allow the knife to encounter the product only. If done correctly, should you slip or cut too closely, the risk of a severe injury is far less. In such a case, only the knuckles will likely be bumped or scraped by the side of the knife. Take your time. This is a skill that must be well practiced before a quick performance is gained.

The Cutting Board:

We can't forget the cutting board. You should note that glass cutting boards should be avoided. They result in loud chopping & could dull or damage your blade. Preferably, a large rectangular wooden or plastic chopping board is best. Place a damp dishcloth or paper towel underneath the board. I find that the plastic shelf lining material is best. This will prevent it from slipping, which will ultimately help prevent finger cuts. Chopping should begin in the center of the board with the knife at a 45-degree angle. This will maximize your work surface and cutting range.

The Right Tools:

The right tool can help to simplify a task. Great tools can lighten a workload, resulting in increased productivity and efficiency. Here are a few to get you started.

Basic Tools:

- Cutting boards (plastic or wood)
- Knives (chef's, paring, serrated, boning + kitchen shears)
- Grater and micro plane
- Whisk
- Rubber spatulas and Wooden spoons
- Tongs
- Metal spatulas
- Sauté pans (1 large, 1 small)
- Pots with lids (1 large, 1 small)
- Sheet pans (rust resistant)
- Glass or stainless-steel bowl set
- Parchment paper
- Colander (1 large)
- Foil
- Fine mesh strainer
- Braising pot
- Casserole baking dishes
- Squirt bottles (cheap and useful)
- Air-tight storage containers
- Zip lock bags

Chapter 4: Methods

Moist Heat Cooking Methods:

- **Baking (surprisingly so)**: Cooking foods, bread, or baked items in moderate heat in the oven. This method could be used in a manner that's either moist or dry heat.
- **Boiling**: Cooking food submerged in a hot liquid (rapidly bubbling liquid at approximately 212° F) which usually cooks food faster.
- **Braising**: A combination cooking method in which foods are usually browned in hot fat, then covered and slowly cooked in a small amount of liquid over low heat.
- **Parboiling**: Partially cooking food in boiling or simmering liquid; similar to blanching but the cooking time is longer.
- **Poach**: Submersion or shallow cooking in liquid; it is a gentler cooking method that uses convection to transfer heat from a hot liquid to a food; often associated with delicately flavored foods that do not require long cooking times to tenderize them (like eggs or fish).
- **Simmer**: Food is submerged in a liquid held at temperatures between 185-205° F; often used with foods that need to be tenderized through long, slow, moist cooking (often used for less tender cuts of meat or to cook soups & sauces).
- **Steam**: Food is usually placed in a basket or rack above a boiling liquid without touching it directly; it should be positioned so that steam is able to circulate around it (helps to enhance a food's natural flavor and helps to retain nutrients).
- **Stewing**: A combination of both dry and moist cooking, where the meat is first browned in a little fat then finished in a liquid or sauce (usually with a shorter cook time than braising).

Dry Heat Cooking Methods:

- **Broiling:** Foods cooked by intense heat radiating from an overhead source.
- **Deep Fry:** Food is submerged in hot fat.
- **Fry**: Food is cooked in hot fat (without full submersion).
- **Grilling**: Similar to broiling but uses a heat source located beneath the cooking surface & the cooking surface is usually in the form of parallel metal bars (gas, electric, wood burning, or charcoal, which adds a smoky flavor).
- **Pan Fry:** Food is cooked in a moderate amount of fat.

- **Poeleing** (pwah-lay-ing): A combination cook method similar to both roasting and braising; the food is cooked in an oven, but in a covered pot with aromatic vegetables and fat/ butter so that it steams in its own juices.
- **Roasting and Baking**: The process of surrounding food with dry, heated air in a closed environment. Roasting is usually applied to meats and poultry. Baking is typically used with fish, fruits, vegetables, starches, bread, or cakes & pastry items.
- **Rotisserie**: Cooking equipment/ technique in which meat or other foods slowly rotate in front of a heating element.
- **Sautéing**: Uses a hot pan with a small amount of hot fat and a food product that isn't damp; usually cooks quickly over high temperatures (don't overcrowd the pan).
- **Searing**: To brown food quickly over high heat; usually done as a preparatory step for combination cooking methods (ex: searing one side of a steak to form an outer crust, then finishing it in the oven).
- **Stir fry**: A variation of sautéing where a wok is used instead of a sauté pan using very high heat, a little fat, and constant stirring.

Chapter 5: What Kind of Cook Are You?

2 Corinthians 13:5

Take a moment to examine what suits your daily schedule? How much time do you have available to prep food each day? While it is certainly acceptable to purchase healthy meal services, this is not feasible for the average household.

If you're unable to hire a cook, you may want to consider doing some meal prep in advance. Again, the more you cook, the more money you can save. As a result, the more control you have over your family's well-being! As my daughter would say, "Make it with love!" Be proud that you're able to nurture them from within.

Step one, let's recognize what works best for you. This is vital for success! In all things, if a new concept seems impossible and inconvenient, you will be less likely to maintain it. Let's narrow that possibility and put the best foot forward.

So….

What kind of cook are you? Are you a busy working mom? You may only have an hour or so to get dinner on the table. Quick and simple is the way to go!

Maybe you're a stay-at-home mom juggling chores and homeschooling? Leave it and forget about it for a length of time may be your mantra. In this case, low and slow is for you!

However, some may prefer to designate one or two days to meal prep for a stress-free week. This would give the assurance that a hot, nutritious meal is already situated. Knocking it out at once would certainly be up your alley!

Now, once you've self-examined and come to know your availability preferences, we can proceed. With these things in mind, you may want to structure your meal prep based on cooking methods that suit your availability needs. See the recommended cooking methods below.

3 Types of Cooks:

- **Quick & Simple:** Stovetop methods, roasting, baking.
- **Low & Slow:** Crockpot meals, soups/ stews, baking & casserole type dishes.
- **Knock It Out At Once:** A combination of cooking methods that will allow for multiple meal concepts to be made at once (baking, roasting, stovetop, crockpot meals and etc.).

Prep for Success:

As mentioned before, set yourself up for success! Arrange your kitchen tools and gadgets according to your cooking method needs.

"(27) Prepare thy work without, and make it fit for thyself in the field; and afterwards build thine house. (32) Then I saw, and considered it well: I looked upon it, and received instruction." Proverbs 24:27, 32

"Hear counsel, and receive instruction, that thou mayest be wise in thy latter end.." Proverbs 19:20

Chapter 6: Let's Cook

"Let all things be done decently and in order." 1 Corinthians 14:40

Now, let's put some of these concepts into practice.

At home, I prefer quick methods of cooking. Most of the meals that I prepare are baked, roasted, or sautéed. However, I also combine cooking methods to utilize the "knock it out at once" theme. This gives me more "kitchen superpower" and flexibility!

Want to gain more efficiency and kitchen superpowers: organizing is key! A great tool learned in culinary school is actually a phrase. **"Mise en place"** is a necessary mindset to adapt. It's a French term meaning everything in its place. Simply put, before beginning a recipe or task, be sure you have all the tools and ingredients needed out and in place. This will save you a lot of time and headaches. You'd hate to get halfway through a recipe to find you're missing an ingredient or necessary tool.

Planning is essential! Write your grocery list. Have a general idea of your weekly menu. This can help to maximize your budget and bring health consciousness to the forefront. This is especially so if you cross-utilize ingredients.

When shopping, allow for 4 to 6 ounces of protein per person in a recipe. Keep it relatively simple. For instance, let's look at the following menu. With this menu, you can almost make two to three meals at once. Be sure to do your "mise en place." Make a prep list in the order they are to be done and check off completed tasks as you go.

You'd be surprised how simple it can be to make half your week's meals in under six hours.

Let's prepare three meals at once.

Below is an example of a full week's menu. This menu is efficient because it cross-utilizes ingredients. This will help you to reduce waste and increase the speed of production. As you proceed, you'll see that I've selected three meals from this menu to guide you through.

Weekly Family Menu (Below is an example)

- **Day 1-** Garlic Chicken w/ Sautéed Zucchini Noodles
- **Day 2-** Citrus Fish Pouch
- **Day 3-** Chicken Cobb Salad
- **Day 4-** (One Pan Bake) Lemon Herb Fish w/ Roasted Rondelle Veggies
- **Day 5-** Chicken Gyros w/ Cous Cous Salad & Fresh Tzatziki Sauce

Keep In Mind:

- Create a menu that cross utilizes ingredients
- Keep it relatively simple
- Don't be afraid to customize and substitute

Citrus Fish Pouch

Chicken Cobb + Vegetarian Cobb with Quinoa

Preparation of Cold Chicken Gyros

Three Meals at Once…

We will focus on three dishes from the suggested menu:

1. Citrus Fish Pouches
2. Chicken Cobb Salad
3. Chicken Gyros w/ Cous Cous Salad and Fresh Tzatziki Sauce

See chapter 12 for the actual recipes. Here, I will coach you through the process.

Remember to portion meats according to your family size.

This alternative is for the more adventurously confident cook. If your time is slim during the week and you cannot afford to hire a chef, this may work for you! Consider making and or prepping a few meal options in advance.

Don't get overwhelmed! Remember, you're in control. The goal is to do a bit of prep ahead to have a simpler, more cost-effective week.

Plan Ahead For Success!

Create your grocery list

Shop and modify as needed. Don't be afraid to make complementary substitutions! See the recipes in chapter 12 in the "Chana's Creations" section.

Set time aside to accomplish the job without interruption.

Set up your kitchen with workstations:

- **Raw Meat Prep Area**- Make certain that this is separate from your veggie prep and other ready-to-eat ingredients (near the sink). Always strive to avoid cross-contamination. Also, clean and sanitize the area afterward.
- **Veggie Chopping Area**- Have the cutting board and sharpened chef's knife out and ready with a trash bowl or bag nearby.
- **Get Your Tools**- Have your skillet out, your pot of water on the stove ready to boil, and the necessary tools out and ready to use. Pre-tear the foil or parchment sheets for the fish pouches. See my YouTube video "How to prep and cook chicken like a pro" for more tips.
- **Prep the Veggies**- Rinse the veggies and herbs that will be used and set them aside.
- **Spices**- Take out the intended seasonings and create the spice blends you expect to use.

Let's Begin…

Begin With the Meats

The simplest way I tackle making multiple entrées at once is to start with the meats! Dealing with raw protein is often the most tedious and time-consuming part of this process.

Keep in mind that poultry and meats have different temperatures of doneness! With this said, you should fabricate the item that has the lowest temperature requirement first. See the chart below…

Internal Cooking Temperatures for Doneness:

- Beef and lamb- 155° F
- Eggs- 145° F, Egg Dishes- 160° F
- Fish- 145° F
- Poultry- 165 ° F
- Stuffed Meats, Filled Pasta/Casserole Dishes, Whole Chicken- 185° F
- Note: Make certain to reheat all cooked foods to an internal temperature of 165°F

Clean and prep one meat at a time. Make sure to wash the sink and workstation in between each meat fabrication (if necessary).

To prep the three entrées, we will work with the fish first. Then, the chicken can be dealt with.

Menu: 3 Meals At Once

Citrus Fish Pouches

Chicken Cobb Salad

Chicken Gyros w/ Cous Cous Salad and Fresh Tzatziki Sauce

The Fish

Clean It- Rinse the fish in a cold water and lemon juice bath.

Set It Aside- Place the cleaned fish on a plate, sheet pan, or dish. Season both sides of the fish with granulated garlic, salt, and pepper (or the Judah blend). Cover it with plastic wrap and place it in the fridge until it's time to assemble the pouches. Be sure to thoroughly wash & sanitize the prep & sink areas afterwards.

The Chicken (For Both the Cobb and the Gyros)

Clean It- Rinse the chicken in cold water and a lemon juice bath. Remember to fabricate enough chicken to accommodate portions for both dishes. See the recipes in chapter 12 in the "Chana's Creations" section.

Pat It Dry- Remember, dry protein will allow for successful browning! Prior to handling the raw chicken, pre-tear several paper towel sheets to pat the poultry dry. This will help reduce the risk of cross-contamination during prep. Should you forget, simply wash up before touching the paper towel roll. See chapter 2 (Sanitation & Food Safety) for tips on handling food safely.

Set It Aside- Place the cleaned and dried chicken on a sheet pan. Season both sides of the chicken with granulated garlic, onion powder, salt, pepper, and chopped herbs. Cover it with plastic wrap and place it in the fridge until it's time to work with it further. Be sure that the chicken is stored below the fish. Remember that the fish requires less time to cook and a lower temperature of doneness to kill harmful bacteria. As always, don't forget to clean & sanitize all affected areas after fabricating the chicken.

Building Your Meal Kits

Prep the Veggies

Rinse It- Rinse all veggies prior to beginning. Dry them or leave them on a clean linen or paper towels to air dry. Remember, moisture can speed up spoilage rates.

Prep and Cut- Chop and slice up your veggies for both the fish pouches and the salad kits. Make certain to have these items ready before assembling the fish pouches.

Finish Prepping the Entrées

For the full recipes, check out chapter 12 in the "Chana's Creations" section.

Keep in Mind- With the meat prep complete, you can simply finish the cold toppings each day before serving dinner. You have begun the start of three-meal kits!

Finishing Up

Finish Your Salad Kit- Fully cook ½ of the prepped & seasoned chicken. Now, you are able to create individual salad bowls or a family salad kit for the next day! Reserve the rest of the chicken for the gyro meal. Store the raw, marinated meat on the lowest shelf on a sheet pan. Or, it can be transferred to a large zip bag and placed in your meat drawer until cooking time.

Quick tip: You can even fully cook all the chicken at once. This is especially so if you plan to serve the chicken gyro meal cold. Just remember to reserve half of the cooked poultry to create that entrée. Be certain to allow the gyro chicken to fully cool before labeling & storing.

Set up Your Fish Pouches and Freeze- Follow the instructions on the recipe for the Citrus Fish Pouches. These convenient bundles can be completely put together from start to finish as custom gourmet frozen dinners. They can be baked in the oven or even cooked directly on a grill. Keep them on hand as a quick "go-to" meal!

The Gyro Kit- Now it's time to use the remaining half of the reserved, prepped and seasoned chicken breasts for the gyro meal. Adjust quantities for your family size. Bake or grill the chicken breast to 165° F internally. If dark meat is used, cook it to 185°F.

When to Serve

Serve The Fresh Veggie Option 1st- Serve the salad meal 1st as it is best eaten freshly made. This will help prevent waste. The lettuce and veggies will begin to wilt or become soggy soon after production. Let's not let your hard work, efforts, and the product go to naught!

Serve The Gyro Kit 2nd- The meat can be marinated for up to 3 days prior to cooking. I recommend leaving this option for mid-week. Avoid spoilage and offer this meal within three days of working with the chicken. Finish the cooking process of the meat the day it's intended to be served. Clean and chop the veggies for this option on the day you plan to serve the fresh chicken gyros. *Quick tip:* Use your time wisely & prepare the accompanying veggies/ side while the chicken bakes.

The Fish Pouches (Serve Anytime) - These are a great freshly made frozen meal! Keep these in your freezer until ready to bake. Just put them on a sheet pan prior to cooking and enjoy them whenever you need a break from kitchen duty!

Chapter 7: Tips for Success

Chef's Tip:

AMP UP THE FLAVOR! One of the most important tips is to build flavor. Browning or caramelization creates a deeper complexity in taste. Toasting spices or even lightly toasting or roasting nuts will also make a strong impact. Likewise, the use of aromatics & fresh herbs can make all the difference in developing full flavor. Soups, sauces, and many dishes start with a foundation of aromatic veggies like onion, garlic, celery, and carrots to boost taste. I like to keep low sodium stock in the pantry as well as keep the basic aromatics on hand.

YOU'VE GOT THE POWER! The more you can make, the more control you have of what you're consuming. Personally, I try to make as much as I can from scratch. Usually, it's more cost-effective, as you will get a greater yield. Believe me, there are times when I take shortcuts. When doing so, be sure to check labels (ensure that it's kosher), choose the best ingredient options within your budget, and amp up the flavor.

Quick Tips:

- *Layer flavors*- season in stages, be careful not to over-salt.
- Use *citric acids*- citruses like lemon and lime hit the pallet like salt; reduce salt usage by adding a bit of citrus juice and flavor packing ingredients like fresh herbs and garlic.
- *Caramelization* (not burnt) - creates flavor & brings out the mild natural sweetness.
- *If you thicken*- once added, thickeners are usually at the full effect when it comes to a boil. This is especially so with the use of flour.
- *When deglazing*- add a cold flavorful liquid like wine or stock to a hot pan; whisk until the browned bits from the bottom of the pan are released and are dissolved and incorporated.

Fat Facts

Let's Talk Fat

Being more active in the kitchen has its advantages. Now, you can control the levels of fat, sodium, and carbohydrates used.

Healthier cooking oils can be used to reduce cholesterol and the absorption of saturated fats. Fat is as essential to your diet as protein and carbohydrates are in fueling your body with energy.

However, the excess calories from eating too much fat of any type can lead to weight gain and be harmful to your heart health over time.

Saturated and trans fats have been identified as potentially harmful to your heart. Most of the foods that contain these types of fats are solid at room temperature (butter, margarine, shortening, and beef/ chicken/ unlawful pork fats and even coconut oil). Butter in the culinary world is vital in certain recipes for the flavor & or richness it provides.

Moderation is key. For daily use, stick with EVOO, light olive or avocado oils to prepare meals. Reserve the butter for specific recipes (unleavened bread, biscuits, a tad for flavor in grits, etc.) and reduce how often these items are consumed. Try modifying your recipes with a healthier substitute by half or entirely (ex. substitute ½ butter required in a quick roux with avocado or olive oil).

Trans-fats are often found in processed foods, fried foods (donuts, French fries, deep-fried fast food), baked goods, and even microwave popcorn. For these reasons, I prefer to make as much from scratch as my budget and time can allow. Claim your kitchen power & choose a healthier fat alternative!

Food for thought…

Did you know that coconut oil is highly unhealthy to eat regularly? While it has several amazing advantages as a topical application (skin, hair or an oral rinse), coconut oil is loaded with saturated fats. Surprisingly so, as it is thought to be a healthy tropical oil. Unfortunately, coconut oil is comprised of over 80% saturated fats & is not optimal for daily consumption. This could certainly clog arteries & raise bad (LDL) cholesterol levels greatly over time. So be mindful, do your research & remember that moderation is key!

Select With Purpose

Keep in mind that certain fats have a low smoke point. The smoke point is the temperature at which the fat or oil begins to smoke and burn. The higher the smoke point, the longer the oil can withstand high cooking temperatures. See the smoke point chart near the back of the book for more info.

When making your oil selection, firstly, consider the cooking method. The cooking method should determine the oil smoke point needed.

For example, when boiling, simmering, or baking, butter or any flavorful oil choice could be used. Yet, the use of oil is likely unnecessary in boiling unless you're looking to add richness. If doing a medium to high heat cooking method such as sautéing, searing, roasting, or braising, avocado, canola, safflower, clarified butter or even olive oils are suitable. When frying, oils with high smoke points and relatively neutral flavor work well (canola, vegetable, or fry oil blends as they aren't excessively expensive). Peanut oil is excellent for frying too, yet it does have a specific flavor and isn't suitable for those with nut allergies. Always consider the final taste, nutritional value, cooking method, cost, and who's consuming it. As I mentioned before, I prefer EVOO for everyday cooking. Afterall, extra virgin olive oil is one of the healthiest options. Not only is EVOO full of antioxidants, but it's loaded with heart-healthy fats and contains vitamins E & K.

Chapter 8: Frying

When Frying: Safety and Preparation

Hot oil can result in potential burns and or fire! Don't worry. This is totally avoidable. Safety is a must! Be sure to utilize a frying skillet or pot tall enough for frying (a deep skillet or 6-quart heavy bottom pot for deep frying or an actual deep fryer). Oil expands when heated to high temperatures and will slightly rise when the food is added in.

Usually, you should allow for about 1 & ½ to 2 inches of oil (about 2-5 cups) for pan-frying. A frying thermometer is recommended. Deep frying is done between 325-375 degrees F. This will vary depending upon the item fried. For thicker cuts of meat (like chicken), a lower range (315-350°F) is more suitable. This will allow for the interior of the product to cook thoroughly before the outside is too brown.

Again, "mise en place!" Be sure everything is prepped and ready to go (product breaded, oil draining area in place, salt to season, separate tools for the raw & cooked if using meat). Remember to avoid cross-contamination between raw meats and ready-to-eat foods.

Before beginning, make sure you have a lid or sheet pan, a box of salt & a fire extinguisher available. If, by chance, there is a flare-up, *DO NOT ADD WATER! Firstly, smother it with a lid or sheet pan. Or, toss salt over it.* Always have a fire extinguisher at hand (it's messy but use it if necessary). It's better to be prepared and ready to solve a potential hazard.

Don't overcrowd the pan!

When frying, searing, or sautéing, be sure not to over-crowd the pan. If this is done with searing or sautéing, the product will steam & not achieve the desired browning. In frying, the oil will not maintain the proper temperature. Instead of crispy quick cooking, it will result in slower cooking with an oily/ soggy product and a crust that will likely not adhere to the food.

Note: Raw garlic burns when fried for longer than about 45 seconds or even less. You can include it in marinades for your meats. Once it marinates, remove the fresh garlic, pat it dry, and season the meat with dry spices before applying your choice of breading. On the other hand, marinated garlic can be fried along with veggies or fish as they cook quickly. Do not fry it with a longer cooking item such as chicken, as it will burn and become bitter. Another option is to simply use granulated or garlic powder on foods that require a longer frying time..

Breading Types:

- **Standard breading procedure** - (results in a relatively thick, crisp coating) a three-step process best-done assembly line style using 3 containers (1 with coating flour, 1 with egg wash, 1 with the final coating):

1. *dry and lightly coat the item in seasoned flour*
2. *quickly dip it in egg wash*
3. *coat in seasoned breadcrumbs or the final breading choice (crushed crackers, cornmeal, panko, ground unroasted nut blend, seasoned flour, etc.)*
4. *once all the desired product is breaded, place it directly into the hot oil to fry or drizzle oil and bake in a 400-degree F preheated oven to oven fry; bake it until the internal temp reaches doneness (see the chart)*
5. *Note: if frying, cook in batches, do not overcrowd the pan*

- **Homestyle dredging**- best applied when dredging damp product; coat moderately with seasoned flour or a ground grain/ breadcrumb mix (brown bag chicken or shake in a zip bag)
- **Battering**- a two to three-step process which uses a batter variation (between pancake to thin crepe batter consistency depending on the desired crust):

Make the Batter:

- *dry food and lightly coat it in flour, shake off excess flour*
- *dip in batter and place the item directly in the hot oil to fry*

Tempura Fried Veggies

Close up

Tempura Breading Station
(from start to finish)

Plated Tempura Veggies with Spicy Asian Hummus

Chapter 9: Nutrition

"A cheerful and good heart will have a care of his meat and diet." Ecclesiasticus 30:25

A more active and mindful role in your kitchen can result in more nutrient-rich foods and fewer empty calories. Also, this gives you the perfect opportunity to reconfigure a fattening favorite into a healthier version.

For instance, you could convert a creamy potpie recipe by altering the bechamel sauce. It could be modified with 2% milk & a 1/4 cup of heavy cream to give that full-fat flavor. Or, you could opt out of using a cream-based sauce and use a classic velouté (flavor-enhanced and thickened stock). You could even use a veggie purée such as seasoned & thinned butternut squash instead. It's all up to the cook!

With this newly claimed kitchen power, you can increase the use of nutrient-rich veggies and fruits. Use the charts below to help you get started.

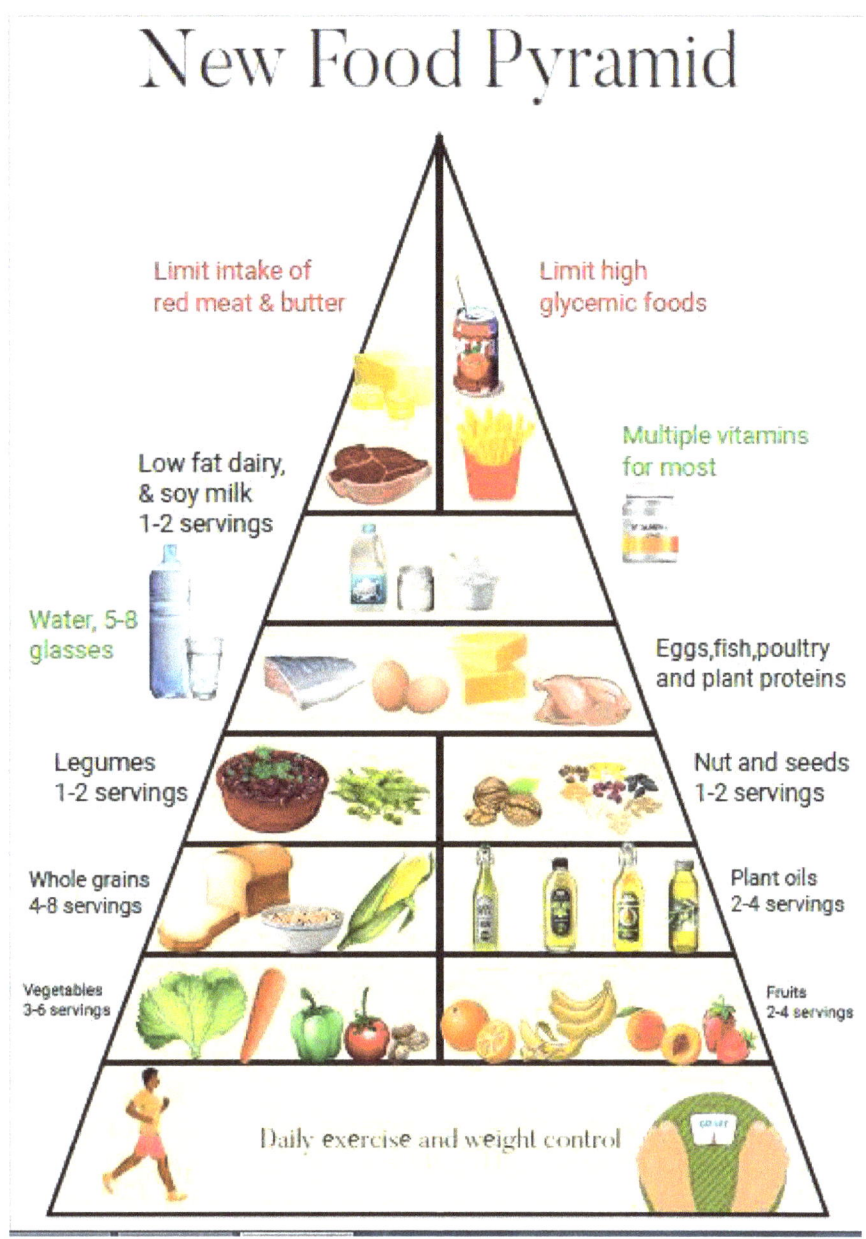

"(16) Eat, as it becometh a man, those things which are set before thee; and devour not, lest thou be hated. (17) Leave off first for manners' sake; and be not unsatiable, lest thou offend." Ecclesiasticus 31:16-17

Chapter 10: Eat To Live and Eat Lawfully

"Keep my commandments, and live; and my law as the apple of thine eye."
Proverbs 7:2

Did you know that eating certain foods could impact you in multiple ways? God created all things and creatures for a purpose. Some are for our benefit, and some are not for consumption. We all should practice maintaining healthy eating habits. God has created the plants of the earth for our nourishment & healing. However, there is a dietary base that those walking in repentance must follow.

According to the Bible, we are not to eat pork, certain land creatures, fish without scales or fins, shellfish, or certain fowl. As quoted in Leviticus chapter 11, "These are the beasts which ye shall eat among all the beasts that are on the earth" God has specified what is lawful for us to consume. See the eleventh chapter of the book of Leviticus for in-depth instructions.

Be mindful at all times of what you or your family eats! Unclean ingredients can be hidden in some packaged food items. So, read carefully! Even vitamins may contain gelatin that is most often made with pork. Be sure that your vitamins and meds, such as pain pills, are without pork-based gelatin or coating. This is why it's so important to expand your culinary abilities. You'll be able to eat more of what you want with the assurance of knowing what it's made of.

Acceptable Meats/ Foods (for those repenting):

"Whatsoever parteth the hoof, and is clovenfooted, and cheweth the cud, among the beasts, that shall ye eat." Leviticus 11:3

- For example, we may eat animals such as cow/ ox, buffalo, bison, lamb & goat because they meet the criteria mentioned above. (Deuteronomy 14:4-6)
- Fish with scales & fins (Leviticus 11:9)
- Lawful Poultry- chicken, turkey & cornish hens (Leviticus 11:21)
- Vegetation- "Every herb bearing seed…for meat" (Genesis 1:29)
- Lawful Bugs- (not that I'd like to eat them) locust, beetles & grasshoppers.

Edible Bugs

"Yet these may ye eat of every flying creeping thing that goeth upon all four, which have legs above their feet, to leap withal upon the earth;" Leviticus 11:21

Let the Pork and Shrimp Go…

We are to be holy, sanctified & not partake in eating abominable foods.

Swine, a.k.a. pork, is a hindrance for some of our people. Yet, it is an abomination to the Lord thy God. Thus, you should not consume it! The word abomination in the Merriam-Webster dictionary means extreme disgust and hatred. I certainly do not want to be considered as such in the eyes of the Lord.

You must "examine yourself" (2 Corinthians 13:5). Is eating bacon, baby back ribs, or shrimp truly worth destroying your health? It is medically proven that these animals cause various ailments in the body. Now that I've learned better, this is an obvious NO for me!

Remember, there are many great alternatives to get that smoky flavor that many of us have become accustomed to. There are even beef or lamb ribs available. In stores today, there are surprisingly good varieties of smoked turkey, beef, and even lamb bacon too. You can even buy liquid smoke to bump up your favorite BBQ recipe. So, scratch that crispy hickory-smoked itch lawfully and be in God's good graces!

"Let us hear the conclusion of the whole matter: Fear God, and keep his commandments: for this is the whole duty of man." Ecclesiastes 12:13

Swine/ Pork Is Unlawful To Eat

Leviticus 11:7-8

"(7) And the swine, though he divide the hoof, and be clovenfooted, yet he cheweth not the cud; he is <u>unclean</u> to you. (8) Of their flesh shall ye not eat, and their carcase shall ye not touch; they are <u>unclean</u> to you."

Other Unacceptable Foods

Leviticus 11:44, 46-47

"(44) For I am the Lord your God: ye shall therefore sanctify yourselves, and ye shall be holy; for I am holy: neither shall ye defile yourselves with any manner of creeping thing that creepeth upon the earth. (46) This is the law of the beasts, and of the fowl, and of every living creature that moveth in the waters, and of every creature that creepeth upon the earth: (47) To make a difference between the unclean and the clean, and between the beast that may be eaten and the beast that may not be eaten."

I encourage you to do your own research on the unclean animals that the Bible lists. Discover for yourself how they could affect your body!

Continue to read Deuteronomy chapter 14 and Leviticus chapter 11 for more in-depth information.

We Are Not To Eat

- The pig/ swine (the earth's garbage disposal)
- The camel (Leviticus 11:4)
- The coney & the hare (Leviticus 11:5-6)
- All sea creatures without scales & fins/ this includes shellfish like shrimp, scallops, mussels, crawfish, clams, catfish, swai & oysters (Leviticus 11:10; *garbage disposals of the sea*)
- The frog (Leviticus 11:42-43)
- Unclean fowls - eagles & their kind, ostrich, ospray, vulture, kite, ravens & their kind, owls & their kind, night hawk, cuckow, the hawk & his kind, cormorant, swan, pelican, stork, heron & her kind, lapwing & the bat (Leviticus 11:13-20)
- weasel, mouse, tortoise, & his kind, ferret, chameleon, lizards, snail & the mole (Leviticus 11:29-31)
- Roadkill- (Leviticus 11:39, Deuteronomy14:21)
- Snakes & lizards (Leviticus 11:42-44)
- Baby cow, aka veal (Deuteronomy 14:21)
- Blood, bloody or undercooked meats (Leviticus 17:14)

"(7) Nevertheless these ye shall not eat of them that chew the cud, or of them that divide the cloven hoof; as the camel, and the hare, and the coney: for they chew the cud, but divide not the hoof; therefore they are unclean unto you. (8) And the swine, because it divideth the hoof, yet cheweth not the cud, it is unclean unto you: ye shall not eat of their flesh, nor touch their dead carcase." Deuteronomy 14: 7-8

Did you know that eating the appropriate foods can alleviate many health issues?

Your body will often show signs of nutrition deficiencies. For instance, leg cramps and fatigue are common during pregnancy. Foods high in potassium can help to relieve this issue (cooked spinach, peas, bananas, etc.). Foods high in iron like dark leafy greens can help to offset anemia when eaten regularly.

Stay full longer with healthy ancient grains such as quinoa, barley, freekeh, or farro. These powerful fiber and protein packing grains can add a nutritional boost to meals throughout your busy week. Also, when you consume foods high in fiber and nutrients, you will have more energy and will be less likely to overeat. Disclaimer, though I am educated in nutrition; I am not a dietitian. Please consult with your doctor before making any diet alterations that could conflict with your medications.

However, in all things, we must remember moderation & that ultimately God controls all.
"For it was neither herb, nor mollifying plaister, that restored them to health: but thy word, O Lord, which healeth all things." Wisdom of Solomon 16:12

What Fresh Foods Can Do?

"The Lord hath created medicines out of the earth; and he that is wise will not abhor them." Ecclesiasticus 38:4

- <u>Hydration-</u> (water, water, water) hydrates the body and reduces contractions, reduces fatigue and heat stroke.
- <u>Extra Protein and Calcium-</u> dark leafy greens, bean & legumes, Greek yogurt with live cultures, items with probiotics, fully cooked eggs.

- *Legumes, Peas, and Beans*- full of fiber, plant protein, iron, folate, potassium, phosphorus, B-vitamins and calcium
- *Whole Grains- Ancient grains are a must! They help lower bad cholesterol & insulin levels. Some examples are* oats, barley, buckwheat, and quinoa-the only grain which is a complete protein.
- *Cruciferous Vegetables Like Broccoli and Dark Leafy Greens*- fiber; vitamin C, K, A, calcium, iron, folate, and potassium (these veggies will help prevent constipation and anemia when eaten regularly and are cancer-fighting coniferous veggies).
- *Lean Meats*- consume fish and poultry (eat red meats less and allow the body to rest from meat consumption from time to time—fast often). Lean meats offer healthy protein & a variety of nutrients
- *Dried Fruits and Nuts*- great portable snacks (cranberries, cherries and apricots can help with urinary tract infections), while nuts, at the least, are a healthy fat full of fiber, other nutrients & protein.
- *Healthy Fats-* Make good choices & select healthy unsaturated fats like olive oil for regular use. Consume more omega 3-fatty acids found in foods like fish, avocado, nuts, flaxseed, chia seeds, seaweed, edamame & even walnuts (fats found in these foods are vital for energy & help to protect heart/ brain health; they can even help to lower bad cholesterol levels, improve memory & reduce the risks of heart disease)

Chapter 11: Prep for Success

Do a little prep to set yourself up for success.

Choose a prep day conducive to your schedule. Set aside a few hours to ensure that you have quick and healthy meal options available.

Reform your mindset to manage prep time. It can be done. This will allow you to better control what you're consuming, even during a hectic week.

Have ready-made meals on hand. I love being able to pull a quick option from the freezer, which I know was made with quality, health-conscious ingredients.

Deal with the meat. Oftentimes, I find that the most difficult part about preparing dinner is cooking the meat. Minimize the stress of this task by getting it oven-ready. If you're a meat-eater, season, marinate and freeze a couple of protein options (Some examples: Cajun marinated chicken breast with thyme/ rosemary and garlic marinated lamb). Put it on oven-ready foil pans or in zip bags. Don't forget to label and date it for future use.

Prep your veggies. Make foil pouches or zip bags of dinner-ready veggies to simplify your busy week. It will make a world of difference for those working or homeschooling moms!

Customize for your family's needs! In doing the prep for yourself, you are actually creating custom options to meet the needs of your family. As a personal chef, I am hired to do exactly that. In simpler terms, I, too, do this for my household.

With the needed basic tools and a few culinary essentials, you, too, will be able to implement some of these techniques. Hopefully, these strategies can help simplify your kitchen and enhance nutritional intake. In doing so, you will customize flavor combinations and dietary needs to your liking. Check out the prep list below with meal possibilities.

Preparation To Do List:

- ***Cook a grain or two*** - boil in water with a pinch of salt (keep it neutral so it can be added to breakfast or lunch).
- ***Clean/ dry/ cut veggies*** – wash, drain, spin salad greens and store in an airtight container; wash, dry, and dice firm veggies like zucchini, carrot, or Brussel sprouts; boil and peel nutrient-rich veggies like beets or sweet potatoes. Be mindful to label, date & use up your prep within 3 to 5 days. Some things like blanched & shocked broccoli could even be frozen.

- *Prep/ season meats* – clean, cut, season, or marinate and store in a zip bag or directly on an oven-ready pan (wrap, label, and freeze or refrigerate); boil a few eggs to add to salads or simply to eat for breakfast.
- *Cook your meat* – Season relatively neutral for versatility. I use garlic, salt, and pepper (or the Judah blend). Season and bake or boil a couple of chicken breasts; season, brown up and drain a pack of ground turkey or beef.

Here are some examples of how to put your prepped items to use during the week.

Breakfast

- Build a Greek yogurt parfait layered with berries, farro, and honey. Top it with crunchy nuts or granola before eating.
- Heat, shell and half the boiled eggs. When ready, top with wilted spinach and cheese or a drizzle of sriracha sauce.
- Prepare small, portioned bags with nuts and dried fruit for quick snacks or breakfast on the go.

Lunch

- Add a ½ cup of cooked and seasoned grains to your favorite salad.
- Build a garden salad with fresh veggies and about 4 oz. of cooked chicken and or cooked ancient grains.
- Make a raw veggie and grain salad (toss tender small, diced veggies with olive oil, salt, pepper, garlic, fresh herbs, lemon juice, and cooked ancient grains; you can even use your favorite prepared dressings like balsamic vinaigrette or Italian dressing instead of the lemon juice and oil).

Dinner

- Add cooked grains to a soup ex: a garlicky Moroccan spiced bean and lentil soup with kale.
- Make loaded veggie tacos (use and reheat the cooked beef; bump up the veggies by adding diced butternut or zucchini squash, sliced mushrooms and peppers; add taco spices and serve with traditional cold toppings of choice).
- Bake one of your marinated meat selections (baked Cajun chicken with succotash salad).

- Bake or grill the rosemary and garlic lamb then serve it with roasted beets and sweet potatoes (bake on separate pans, cut the parboiled veggies into large dices or wedges before baking, season and toss with olive oil; garnish the lamb with fresh chopped rosemary and lemon zest when served).

Chapter 12: Recipes & More

Upcoming Contents:

- Essentials and Tips
- Spice Blends
- Chana's Creations
- Useful Charts

Essentials and Tips:

- Quick Roux
- Boil Perfect Eggs
- Stock
- The Top 3 Mother Sauces
- Compound Butter
- Sautéing and Searing
- Perfectly Cooked Rice

Quick Roux

Typically, a roux is made directly in the pot per recipe. The ratio is equal parts fat to equal parts flour. It is usually cooked to one of the three stages (white, blonde, or brown). The darker it is cooked, the less thickening power the roux has. As it darkens, the flavor becomes richer & nuttier.

This makes all the difference in classic dishes like gumbo!

However, when I am not utilizing a roux for its flavor profile, I use a quick roux (similar to a beurre manie). I find it much easier and more convenient to make small batches of roux ahead. This allows me to have it on hand as a quick thickener.

But, the raw flour taste must be cooked out. When using a roux, it must come to a boil to reach its full thickening ability. So, adjust accordingly. Note: this is also the case with using a flour slurry.

Ingredients:
- ½ cup A.P. Flour
- ¼ cup olive oil (EVOO)
- ¼ cup unsalted butter (½ stick)

Procedure:
- Melt the butter in a small pot or in the microwave
- Add the olive oil to the butter
- Gradually add flour to the fats, whisking continuously or until combined into a paste
- Cool, store in an air-tight container and label (keep refrigerated)

A Sabbath Breakfast Spread: boiled eggs, turkey bacon, turkey patties, beef sausages, spinach apple drink & cold coffee

Perfectly Boiled Eggs

Boiling eggs seem so simple, right... Sometimes the simplest things are not always easy to achieve. But, with a few easy steps, you too can make beautifully cooked hard-boiled eggs.

In this case, the quantity isn't a factor. Technically, this basic task is method-based. The cook time will vary depending on the number of eggs used. The more eggs cooked, the longer it will take for the water to reach boiling point. So, this is truly a foolproof strategy. Simply put, the fewer eggs, the shorter the cooking time.

You'll need:
- 1 small to a medium pot with a lid
- 4-12 eggs in the shell (or desired quantity)
- Tap water
- 1 Storage container and paper towels

Put the cold raw eggs in a pot. Cover them with cold water. Leave it uncovered and bring the eggs to a boil. Once the boiling begins, allow the eggs to cook for 5 minutes. After 5 minutes, turn off the heat and put the lid on the pot. Let it stand for 3-5 minutes in the hot water.

Now, carefully drain the hot water off the eggs by holding the lid ajar. Put the lid back on the pot and gently rattle the eggs around until the shells are thoroughly cracked. Add a few cubes of ice to stop the cooking and cold water to nearly cover. Now, the shells should peel right off. Pat your perfectly boiled eggs dry and allow them to cool to room temperature before storing and refrigerating.

Stock

A **stock** is a flavorful liquid made from roasted bones and aromatic vegetables. It is a vital flavor base in soups, sauces, braising liquids, and more. What makes a stock different from a broth is simple. A **broth** is not made with roasted bones. Thus, it does not have the deep rich flavor that a stock offers. Nor does it have the gelatinous properties which comes from the bone marrow. So, if time permits, I always prefer the use of stock.

While at the grocery store, see your butcher. They will likely have bones available for purchase. These are usually cheap! You should be able to get your hands on fish, chicken, beef, or even lamb bones.

If you are de-boning at home, keep those bones for stock. Freeze them for another day. Or, go ahead and roast them off while you're taking care of other kitchen tasks! You could always finish the stock process on a more convenient prep day! At any rate, it must have some form of aromatic vegetables. Classically, these veggies would include a **mirepoix** (50% onion, 25% carrot & 25% celery) and a bit of caramelized tomato paste. This particular blend offers a distinct robust flavor. Here's how to make it.

Ingredients:
- Chicken bones (about 1-2 lbs)
- 1-2 large onions
- About 3 qts. water (need a 6-8 qts.. Pot)
- 2 carrots
- 2 celery stalks
- 3 stalks of parsley and thyme
- Spices (2 bay leaves, 2-4 garlic cloves, 1 tsp peppercorns; cloves are classically used)
- 2 tbsp. tomato paste (optional)

Procedure:
- Roast the unseasoned bones in an oven preheated to 350° F to 375° F.
- Cook the bones until they have browned and the blood has cooked off.
- Large dice the onion, carrot, and celery.
- To avoid extra dishes, just add the veggies to the pan of bones when the bones are beginning to brown and are about halfway cooked.
- Roast until both the veggies and bones have caramelized to a nice dark brown around the edges.
- If using tomato paste, stir it around on the cooked veggies and bones at this stage.
- Cook for about 5 more minutes in the oven to allow the tomato paste to caramelize.
- Remove the pan from the oven & add the hot bones and veggie mixture to a large stockpot.
- Deglaze the sheet pan with about ½ cup of water to pull up the **fond** or brown bits. Pour this into the stockpot.
- Using cold water, cover the mixture until the water is about an inch away from the top.
- Add the spices loosely or either in a "sachet" or "bouquet garni."
- Bring it to a boil, then reduce the heat to allow the stock to simmer (small bubbles form around the edge of the pot; not boiling).

- NEVER let your stock boil after this phase.
- Allow it to simmer gently for about 1-2 hours. It will take longer for a large batch.
- Skim the scum during this process. **Scum** refers to the foamy impurities that float up to the top during cooking. To skim, simply use a ladle & carefully scrape the impurities off of the top as they appear throughout the cooking process. You should have a container of water on hand for this. Keep in mind that the dipping water should be changed as needed. Dip your ladle in the clean water bowl before removing a new scoop of scum. This will help prevent cloudy stock.

Once complete, strain, cool, store, and label. You could divide it up into 3 or 4 air-tight containers for quick use. Or even freeze some in an ice cube tray for easy usage in small-batch sauces, etc. It's up to you…

Skim the Scum (shown above is the removal of the impurities from a pot of stew)

The Top 3 Mother Sauces
Culinary Awareness

As a beginning culinary student, one of the first things taught are the 5 mother sauces. Bechamel, Espagnole, Hollandaise, Velouté & Tomato are necessary for a chef's training. These are used as a base for many dishes ranging from a huge array of sauces to soups and even stews. Without a doubt, the mother sauces are key elements to learn. However, for more practical "everyday cooking," I find 3 to be vital. Bechamel, Tomato & Velouté are the top 3 mother sauces that I seem to use most.

Bechamel*- a thickened cream sauce:*
Often used in creamy soups, cream-based sauces, or creamy casserole dishes such as mac and cheese.

Simple Tomato*- an enriched tomato purée:*
Usually, this is a simple sauce made with crushed tomatoes, water, a pinch of sugar, fresh herbs, salt, pepper and garlic. Often used in many Italian or Mediterranean dishes, classic Italian casseroles such as lasagna & even some soups.

Velouté*- an enhanced & thickened chicken broth or stock:*
Usually used as a base in several soups, sauces, or even casserole dishes, such as some pot pie variations.

Compound Butter

While the use of butter is not the healthiest choice, it certainly packs a big flavor. You can splurge and offer this indulgent condiment on a special occasion. One of God's High Holy Days would certainly be suitable!

It's super easy to create your own flavor-packing compound butter! You can simply add flavorful ingredients to a stick of softened butter. Account for about 2 tbsps. per person to gauge how many sticks of butter you'll need to use. See below for a few awesome suggestions.

Compound Butter Combinations: All should include a pinch of sea salt. Salt enhances all things, even sweets.

Can that which is unsavoury be eaten without salt? Or is there any taste in the white of an egg? Job 6:6

Cinnamon Raisin- finely chopped raisins (that have been rehydrated & strained) with cinnamon & brown sugar.

Rosemary, Garlic, and Lemon- fresh rosemary, fresh minced garlic, lemon zest and juice, S&P.

Passover Blend- with bitter herbs of cilantro, mint, parsley (parsley is not an actual bitter herb but added for its freshness), orange zest, S&P.

Spicy Lime and Thyme- lime zest and juice, crushed pepper flakes, a dash of cayenne, fresh chopped thyme leaves, S&P.

Roasted Garlic & Herb- roasted garlic with a variety of fresh savory herbs with S&P.

Smoky Chipotle and Honey- puréed chipotle in adobo, raw honey, salt, and a pinch of cinnamon.

Sautéing & Searing

Sautéing and searing are dry heat cooking methods. These require moderate to high heat, a small amount of oil, and adequate food spacing. If you prefer a quick, hands-on cooking technique that results in a nicely browned crust, this is the method for you!

Searing is usually used to caramelize the outer skin or flesh of meats or vegetables. In most cases, it involves a two-step cooking process. For example, one may sear ox tails quickly to brown. Then braise them in broth & herbs to be covered to cook slowly in the oven.

Tips For Successful Sautéing & Searing:

- **Avoid Overcrowding-** Overcrowding the pan will simulate a form of steam. You will get minimal, if any, browning at all. Space items out at least ½ inch apart in the pan to avoid this.
- **Use High Heat-** If quick browning is your goal, don't be afraid to crank up the heat! You're in control and could always moderate the heat by turning the flame down if needed. Using high heat will actually allow you to control the level of browning without overcooking the item.

- **Don't Play with It-** To achieve that beautiful, caramelized color, you must leave it to brown. This is especially so with proteins such as fish or chicken. You'd be surprised to find out that once developed, the crust will release itself from the pan. Thus, you will be less likely to break up your protein and reduce losing that lovely crusty skin. This concept also applies to grilling.
- **Preheat the Pan 1st-** Before adding the oil and potentially smoking up the kitchen, preheat your pan. Try using an oil with a higher smoke point. Avocado, canola, coconut, grapeseed, or even peanut oils will do.
- **Start and Finish Differently**– Take control and make it work for you! Sautéing and searing are excellent methods to use to brown meat 1st at high heat and finish it in another way. You could sear off your seasoned meat earlier in the week (Making sure to not cook it all the way through). Then, it could easily be cooled and set up for a meal to finish later in the week. I absolutely love having a few quick meal alternatives waiting in my freezer. We all have those unexpected, chaotic days! Once ready to complete, it's quite easy to add a little broth, a few fresh herbs, and quick cooking veggies then throw the pan into a preheated oven to bake. Just like that, dinner prep could be minutes away.

***Chef's Tip: Should you choose to partially cook your meat for another day, you must cool & store it properly!** Just make sure that you cool it to room temperature before refrigerating. This should all be done within a 2-hour range to avoid time-temperature abuse (see Chapter 2 for more details). Also, store it on the lowest shelf in your fridge to avoid contamination (away from ready to eat foods as it isn't fully cooked).*

Perfectly Cooked Rice

Making a perfect pot of fluffy rice can be a challenge for some. Though seemingly simple, many factors could cause a great or poor result. Let's get down to the basic principles to ensure a perfect pot of rice every time!

Like many other grains, a key factor in preparation lies in the use of proper ratios. Apply this method to prepare rice or ancient grains like quinoa. Always remember the 1, 2, 3 ratio (one part grain, two parts liquid, equaling a 3 part yield). Simply put, for every cup of rice, a doubled amount of liquid should be used. Yes, it could sound complicated. But, perfectly cooked rice is one of the easiest things to make!

Just remember to use the same measuring tool for both the rice & the liquid. This ensures equal volumes as this is ratio based. For instance, to cook one cup of rice, you'll need 2 cups of broth, this will give a final yield of 3 cups cooked rice.

Now, let's consider the next important step to cooking rice: *proper method*. Using the correct method is just as important as the ratio. Let's assume that two cups of uncooked rice is needed. This will give a final portion of 6 cups cooked rice. To start, rinse the measured rice under cold water. Do this until the water becomes nearly clear.

Now, add the cleaned rice to a pot. Add four cups of liquid (water, broth or stock). Season it as desired. Firstly, bring it to a rapid boil. Now, put on the lid & turn the flame down to low. Finally, allow the rice to gently steam for at least 18 minutes before checking. Remember, adequate steaming is pivotal! So, avoid opening the pot during this time frame. Check it for doneness as it may take up to 25 minutes to fully cook. When ready, fluff it with a tad bit of EVOO & adjust the seasonings if needed. Voila, your perfectly cooked rice is ready!

You'll need:
- 1 medium pot with a lid
- 2 cups or portions of long-grain rice (or desired quantity)
- 4 cups tap water or a flavorful liquid
- Spices & desired aromatics tt (s & p, garlic, bay leaf, butter, etc.)
- Note: Different rice varieties may vary in cook times (Jasmine rice may cook faster- in about 16 minutes, whereas wild or brown rice may take longer than the times mentioned above). If you tend to overcook rice, try using par-boiled varieties instead.

Follow the previous instructions to make an easy dinner side, a perfect pot of rice!

Seasoned White Rice with Garlic & Thyme

Spice Blends

Make it your way: You can always create the spice blends to exclude salt to lower sodium. Or, just add the salt to taste afterward (literally, taste a pinch to ensure balance). Store them in airtight containers & remember to label.

- BBQ Rub
- Cajun/ Creole
- Chili
- Curry Fusion
- Flavored Salt
- Italian
- Jerk
- Judah Blend
- Kicking Taco
- Lemony Ranch
- Lemon & Thyme Salt
- Montreal Steak
- Moroccan
- Old Bay
- Oriental Express
- Old Bay Mix
- The Gad Blend
- Smoky Blackening

BBQ Rub: about 2 tbsp. each of granulated garlic and smoked paprika, + ¼ cup light brown sugar + 1 tsp each of thyme, cayenne, chili powder, onion powder and cumin + 1 tsp sea salt & black pepper + ½ tsp of cinnamon.

Cajun/ Creole: 2 tbsp each of paprika & granulated garlic + 1 tbsp each of onion powder, oregano, thyme, black or white pepper + 1 tsp each of sea salt, cayenne, cumin & smoked paprika (optional).

Chili: 4 tbsp. chili powder, 2 tbsp. each of cumin and raw sugar + 1 tbsp. each of chipotle powder or ancho chili powder, onion powder, granulated garlic + 2 tsp each of parsley, oregano and sea salt + ¼ tsp each of cayenne, coriander and cocoa powder.

Note: to the chili spice blend, add ¼ cup of AP flour or corn starch if you'd like it to assist in thickening.

Curry Fusion: 2 ½ tsp turmeric, 1 tsp each white pepper, ginger, mustard powder + ½ tsp each of thyme, cayenne, cumin, coriander, pink salt, sugar + ¼ tsp each of onion powder, nutmeg, cinnamon + 1/8 tsp smoked paprika + 1 ½ tsp granulated garlic.

Flavored Salt: 4 tbsp. sea salt and your choice of 2 tbsp. of fresh chopped herb (you can add 1 tsp of complimenting citrus zest); allow the fresh herbs to dry out in the salt uncovered. This may take about 2-4 days.

Italian: 3 tbsp. each of parsley, basil, oregano and granulated garlic + 1 tsp each of onion powder, thyme and rosemary + ½ tsp each of red pepper flakes and black pepper.

Jerk: 1 tbsp. each of parsley, granulated garlic, brown sugar and onion powder + 2 tsp each of cayenne or scotch bonnet powder, paprika and smoked sea salt + 1 tsp each of black pepper and thyme + ½ tsp each of red pepper flakes, cumin, nutmeg, allspice and cinnamon. Optional ginger powder (tt) is a great addition.

Judah Blend: (my house blend)- 2 tbsp. granulated garlic, 2 tbsp. black pepper, 1 tsp sea salt, ½ tsp granulated onion powder.

Kicking Taco: 2 tbsp. each of granulated garlic, onion powder and chili powder + 1 tsp each of cumin, oregano and paprika + ½ tsp each of sugar, chipotle powder, ancho chili powder and sea salt.

Lemony Ranch: 2 tbsp. parsley, 1 tbsp. each of dill, granulated garlic & onion powder + 2 tsp sea salt + 1 tsp each of black pepper, nutritional yeast and lemon zest.

Lemon & Thyme Salt: 4 tbsp. coarse sea salt, 1 tbsp. fresh thyme leaves (about 6 sprigs), zest of 1 lemon.

Montreal Steak: 2 tbsp. each of crushed or course black pepper, granulated garlic, sea salt (or kosher), paprika plus 1 tbsp. each of onion powder, coriander, dill & crushed pepper flakes.

Moroccan: 2 tbsp. smoked or sweet paprika + 1 tbsp. each of cumin and coriander + 1 ½ tbsp. raw sugar + 2 tsp sea salt + 1 tsp each of cardamom, cinnamon, cloves, nutmeg, cayenne, and granulated garlic.

Old Bay Mix: **5** ground bay leaves, equal parts or about ½ tbsp of each of the following: black pepper, smoked paprika, mustard powder, ground celery seed, cayenne plus ¼ tsp each of nutmeg, cinnamon, cardamom, allspice, and ginger; add 1 to 2 tsp of sea salt to taste (or kosher salt). For more heat, add ½ tsp crushed red pepper flakes

Oriental Express: equal parts ground ginger, coriander, granulated garlic, and onion powder; half part cardamom & cumin, + add salt and white pepper to taste.

The Gad Blend: equal parts of granulated garlic, ground cumin or sage with salt and pepper (or crushed pepper flakes) added to taste.

Smoky Blackening: 2 tbsp. creole spice blend + 1 tbsp. each of smoked paprika and raw sugar + ½ tsp each of cinnamon, thyme, and smoked salt.

Chef's Tip: Don't be afraid to adjust these blends to your liking; customize! *As you make your gourmet spice blends, simply taste a pinch & tweak it as you see fit.*

My Creations and Easy Classics

Here are a few recipes which I have created for personal chef menus. Oftentimes, I develop recipes in this manner.

I get inspired from images or menu concepts and simply create my own variations utilizing the techniques and basic cooking methods discussed in this booklet. You too should not be afraid to get inspired. I welcome you to modify my creations to suit your family's needs.

Remember, if you know basic cooking principles, cooking methods, techniques, and know how to apply them… you are nearly capable of making anything!

My Creations

- Albino Chili
- Anna Gad's Fry Bread (a featured bonus)
- Brown Sugar Bourbon Hens
- Beef & Beer Cheddar Soup
- Black-Eyed Pea Medley
- Cajun Seared Fish with Herbal Purée
- Cajun Butter
- Citrus Fish Pouch
- Chicken Cobb Salad
- Chicken Gyros with Tzatziki & Cous Cous Salad
- Chicken Piccata (my way)
- Easy Chicken & Split Pea Soup
- Fried Rice Your Way
- Fried Green Tomatoes
- Garlicky Sautéed Quick Greens
- Hummus Your Way
- Simple Sautéed Asparagus or Green Beans
- Smoky Garlic & Quinoa Salad
- Spicy Asian Kale & Cucumber Salad
- Southern Sweet Cornbread
- Stuffed Zucchini Logs with Marinara

- Sweet Potato Mash
- Whole Split Chicken & Parmesan Creamed Spinach

Albino Chili

Yields: about 6-8 portions

Ingredients

- 1 large poblano (seeded & diced)
- 1 to 2 jalapeno or serrano chiles (seeded & finely diced)
- 3-4 garlic cloves (minced)
- 1 lb. ground turkey
- 2 parsnips (peeled & diced)
- 2 cans white beans (drained & rinsed)
- ½ jar salsa verde (about 3 oz)
- 4 cups chicken stock
- ½ cup white wine or light beer
- 4-6 tbsp of quick roux
- Olive oil as needed
- About 1 tsp lime juice (tt)
- 4 tbsp cilantro (chopped)

Note: You will need 4-6 tbsp. of quick roux (see the quick roux recipe in the Essentials & Tips section).

Spices: granulated garlic, 1 bay leaf, onion powder, coriander, cumin, a pinch of cayenne, salt & pepper tt

Tools Needed

A large 4-6 qtr. Pot and lid, a cutting board/chef's knife, a colander, a can opener, a wooden spoon, or a rubber spatula.

Method

- Rinse and drain the beans and set them aside.
- Clean and chop all the veggies to medium dice, and set aside.
- Brown the turkey in a drizzle of EVOO. Be sure to get dark brown bits of caramelization, it makes all the difference in the final flavor!
- Season with the spices as its browning.

- Add half of all the veggies and sauté them for about 3 minutes or until slightly tender. For increased spiciness, don't discard the seeds in the chilies before chopping.
- Add the salsa verde, the garlic and half of the chopped cilantro.
- Allow it to cook for about 1 minute.
- Deglaze the pan with the wine or beer.
- Allow it to evaporate until it is nearly gone while scraping up the brown bits (the fond).
- Add the stock and about 1 cup of water.
- Whisk in about 3 tbsp of quick roux.
- Allow it to come to a boil to determine the final thickness achieved.
- If it has not become your desired thickness, add 1 tbsp of quick roux at a time until it is to your liking. Remember that the roux must come to a boil before it reaches its full thickening power.
- Simmer on medium-low for about 30 minutes.
- Add the remaining veggies and the beans.
- Stir, taste & add more spices as desired.
- This may take an additional 15 minutes to fully develop- Stir occasionally during this process. You want to make sure that there are no clumps of roux floating about. Also, it needs to simmer for the flavors to meld together, bloom, and cook the raw flour taste out.
- Finish the chili with a tsp or so of lime juice.
- A pinch of sugar or agave may be needed to balance out the flavors. It's up to you!
- Garnish with the remaining cilantro & a dollop of sour cream or diced avocado.

This dish would be great served with fresh country cornbread, corn chips, or even a sprinkle of queso fresco.

Fry Bread Pics

Anna Gad's Fry Bread

Served As Gadite Style Buffalo Tacos

Thanks Anna for allowing me to include your recipe!

Yields: about 6-8 large tacos

Tools needed: chef's knife/ cutting board, rolling pin, bowls, spoons, a large frying pan, a large skillet, a clean kitchen towel, a small sauce pot, a draining rack or paper towel lined sheet pan, measuring spoons, dry & liquid measuring cups

Ingredients:

For The Toppings

- 1 tsp fresh sage (chopped) + extra whole leaves for garnish
- 1 tsp fresh rosemary (chopped)
- Fruity red wine (as needed)
- 2 standard cans of refried beans (vegetarian)
- 6 leaves fresh dandelion (shredded)
- 3 green onions a.k.a. scallions (chopped)
- Spices: 1 tsp each of chili powder, cumin, steak seasoning, s & p tt

For The Sauce

- 1 cup blueberry/ peach jam
- 1 large dried smoky ancho chili (soaked)
- ¼ cup red wine
- ½ lime (juice)

Add all the sauce ingredients to a blender & purée until smooth. Simmer until it has thickened; set aside

The Fry Bread

- 3 cups loosely packed AP flour
- 1 cup warm water
- ¼ tsp corn oil (add to the warm water)
- 2 tbsp baking powder
- 1 tsp sea salt

Method and Procedure

(The Fry Bread)

- Begin with making the dough.
- Combine all the dry ingredients, stir
- Add the warm water & oil mixture
- Lightly stir until a ball is formed
- Cover it with a lightly dampened kitchen towel
- Let the dough ball rest until it rises. 6 to 8 hours is best (a slower rise will develop better flavor & result in a more tender, delicate fry bread)
- When the dough does not spring back, it's ready!
- Portion the dough into 6 or 8 balls. Stretch them out into elongated oval shapes (use a rolling pin or, for a more authentic look- do it by hand). Don't worry if a hole is made while stretching!
- Preheat 2 cups of corn oil in a large frying pan
- Fry them on medium-high heat for about 1 to 2 minutes on each side.
- When done cooking the bread, go the extra mile & fry some fresh sage leaves. They make an excellent final garnish!

(For The Toppings)

- Using a large skillet, begin to brown the ground buffalo meat. This can be substituted with ground poultry, ground beef, or even mushrooms for a tasty vegan approach.
- As it cooks, season it tt with the spices & fresh herbs mentioned. Deglaze the pan with a few splashes of red wine (about ¼ cup). Keep it on low to stay warm
- In a small sauce pot, fully heat the refried beans. You may need to add a splash of water or broth to slightly thin it out. Season it with the listed spices. Note- Make them spicy! The heat is a delightful bonus to the final dish.
- Wash, dry & chop the fresh dandelion leaves & the scallions as instructed.

(Taco Assembly)

Top each goldenly cooked fry bread with a layer of spicy beans. Add the warm buffalo meat & drizzle on the blueberry sauce. Dress each taco with the dandelion shred & the chopped green onions. Garnish with the crispy fried sage. Enjoy!

Bourbon Hen

Bourbon Hen – Family Style

Brown Sugar Bourbon Hens

Yields: about 6 portions

This pairs perfectly with the simple sautéed asparagus and sweet potato mash.

Ingredients

- 3 each Cornish hen
- 2 oz. bourbon (optional)
- About 2 cups chicken stock
- About 2 cups water
- ¼ cup lemon juice or vinegar
- 3 tbsp. butter (optional)
- About 4 tbsp. olive oil

Spices: About ½ tsp each of cinnamon, cumin, onion powder, and smoked paprika. About 4 tbsp. of bourbon spice rub, 3-4 tbsp. brown sugar, salt, and pepper to taste (blend all the components except the salt to make a rub, taste it first and add salt to your liking—about ½ tsp or so).

Tools Needed: Kitchen shears, 2 tongs (to handle the raw meat & one for the cooked hens), a large sheet, 2 small bowls, aluminum foil (if needed), and 2 small spoons.

Method and Procedure

- Make the spice rub. Note: any excess can be stored for another day (do not contaminate it).
- Clean your sink area and prepare a trash bag/ bowl or bring the trash can nearby.
- Put the sheet pan near the sink area.
- In one sink, fill it halfway with cold water and add about ¼ cup of vinegar.
- Leave the opposite sink clean and empty.
- Remove the innards/ guts from each hen; discard the innards.
- Clean the thawed hens by rinsing them in lemon or vinegar water. Leave them to soak as the others are cut in half.
- Place a hen, one at a time, in the empty sink; flip the hens over.
- Use the kitchen shears to carefully cut each hen in half. Trim off any unwanted excess.
- While working, be mindful not to tear the top skin which covers the breast and thigh meat.
- As each hen is cleaned and cut, place the halves on the nearby sheet pan, flesh side up.

- Careful not to drip the raw poultry liquid everywhere. Remember to try to contain what you are doing to minimize splashing. You want to prevent spreading germs throughout the kitchen. Only work on the raw poultry during this process. To do this, try to have all things on hand before beginning. It is essential that you avoid and or minimize cross-contamination. This is important to remember while handling the raw poultry.

- Once done with all the birds, discard the raw scraps and thoroughly wash your hands (using antibacterial soap and lathering for about 20 seconds in very warm water). Also, thoroughly wash and sanitize the sink and all work areas where you handled the hens. Safety first & remember to tidy as you go!

- Preheat the oven to 375°F.

- Season each hen generously with the spice blend on both sides, leaving the skin side up.

(Note- Keep your hands clean, use the tongs to flip the hens to season the other side).

- Drizzle extra virgin olive oil all over the tops of the hens.

- Combine the bourbon in the 2 cups of stock and pour it on an empty spot on the sheet pan, add the butter nub as well.

- Place the pan in the center of the oven (not on the lowest rack).

- It may take anywhere from 45 minutes to an hour or so for them to fully cook.

- During the baking process, baste each hen with the bourbon stock drippings as they cook.

- If they begin to get golden before close to being done, tent the hens loosely with foil to help avoid burning or bitterness. Remember to baste them about every 15 minutes during cooking.

- Cook the hens until they have reached an internal temperature of doneness of 185°F in the thigh and wing area. Allow them to rest for about 3-5 minutes before serving. If you would like extra bourbon sauce, simply deglaze the pan drippings by adding a bit more stock or water to the sheet pan. Scrape the brown bits & cooking liquids into a small pot. Make sure that there's about 1 cup of liquid in total (stock or water). Add ¼ to ½ cup of bourbon, 2-4 tbsp of brown sugar, about 1 tsp or so of quick roux, a sprig of thyme & season tt with the spice mix. Bring it to a boil, then simmer to let the flavors bloom. Once it's sauce consistency (nappe), whisk in a nub of butter, strain & it's ready! Pair the hens with the sweet potato mash and the simple sautéed asparagus. Even candied pecans sprinkled on top would be a bonus. Enjoy!

Beef & Beer Cheddar Soup
(Personal Chef Style)

Beef & Beer Cheddar Soup

Yields: about 6 portions

Ingredients:

- 1 box beef stock
- 16 oz. sliced mushrooms
- 1 lb. ground angus beef
- 1 qtr. Heavy cream or half & half
- ¼ cup blonde roux or quick roux (equal parts heated fat & flour)
- ½ cup green bell pepper (diced)
- Spices to taste: garlic, onion, s & p, steak spice
- 1 bay leaf
- 1 to 2 bottles of dark beer
- ½ pk turkey bacon (diced)
- 4 sprigs of fresh thyme
- 3 cloves garlic (minced)
- 1 poblano (seeded & diced)
- 2 stalks of celery (diced)
- 1 jalapeño (seeded & diced)
- Cheeses: about 1/3 cup smoked gouda, 1/3 cup dubliner, 2 cup cheddar

Procedure:

- On medium/ high heat, render and lardon the turkey bacon in about 1 tbsp. EVOO until crisp; drain and set aside.
- Add the beef to the same pan, season, and brown; set aside.
- Pour out the excess beef fat, add 1tbsp EVOO and the mushrooms, season, and brown them.
- Remove the mushrooms and set them aside.
- Lower the heat and add the diced veggies and minced garlic; season lightly tt with s & p and cook until tender.
- Deglaze the pot with beer, scrape up the fond (browned bits) and reduce by half.
- Add the stock, bay leaf, and beef; simmer on low for about 15 minutes.

- Add the cream and half of the mushrooms, thicken the soup to your desired consistency with the quick roux (see essential recipes).
- Raise the temperature for about 2 minutes; once it has come to a boil, you can determine if the soup has thickened to your liking. Keep in mind that it will become slightly thicker once the cheese is added.
- Reduce the heat again and allow it to simmer on low for at least 10 minutes
- Add the cheeses and whisk until melted.
- Taste and adjust the seasonings if needed.
- If it is too thick, simply add a bit of stock or cream to achieve your desired consistency.
- Serve hot and top each bowl with a sprinkle of the crispy turkey bacon pieces, some of the browned mushrooms & your choice of cold toppings.

This soup is fun to serve with warm, soft pretzels for dipping. You can also have several cold toppings on the side for your guests or family to customize their bowls.

Fun Optional Toppings (all are not included on the ingredient list):
- Fresh sliced jalapeño
- Sliced green onion (scallions)
- Shredded cheese
- Crispy turkey bacon bits
- Sour cream
- Sautéed peppers & mushrooms
- Caramelized pearl onions
- Extra seasoned and cooked beef or steak strips

Have fun and make it your own!

Seared Fish

Boost your omega 3 fatty acids & vitamin E – keep the skin!

For crispy skin fish: Cook the skin-on fish skin side down 2/3rds of the way before flipping. Serve it skin side up to maintain the crispy skin.

Process of making the herbal purée – pairs nicely with the cajun seared fish with bep medley

Cajun Seared Fish Pic Featuring the BEP Medley (PC Plating)

Black-Eyed Pea Medley

Yields: about 6-8 portions

This side pairs perfectly with the seared Cajun fish!

Ingredients

- 2 cans (vegetarian) black-eyed peas (BEP)
- 1 (16 oz) bag of baby spinach (fresh, not frozen)
- 3 cloves finely minced garlic
- 1 red bell pepper, small diced
- 1 red onion, small diced
- About ¼ cup extra virgin oil
- Spices: Cajun blend, garlic, salt & pepper tt

Tools Needed

- A 14" to 16" skillet (larger is better)
- A sheet pan or full steam table pan
- A rubber spatula or wooden spoon
- Cutting board/ chef's knife
- Strainer/ can opener

Method & Procedure

- Rinse and drain the peas and set them aside.
- While the peas drain, begin to prep the veggies.
- This is a simple recipe but is done best using a multi-step cooking process. This will allow the spinach and veggies to remain green & vibrant. Have a sheet pan or empty prep pan ready.
- Using a large skillet, heat on medium-high heat and begin to sauté the BEP in about 2 tbsp of extra virgin olive oil (EVOO).
- Season to taste with the spices mentioned above.
- Sauté until the moisture is gone and they are slightly browned. They may begin to pop a bit. This is ok.
- Add half of the minced garlic, stir and allow it to cook until the garlic begins to turn golden.

- Pour the BEP onto the empty pan.
- Add more EVOO to the skillet and turn it to high.
- Quickly sauté the onions and peppers. You only want to brown them slightly but not cook them to the point that they lose color and crunch.
- Once slightly browned, add the remainder of the garlic and stir.
- The next step must be done quickly… So, make sure everything is in reach and ready to use.
- Quickly add another tbsp or so of EVOO to the pan and begin to add the spinach to wilt (season).
- Once the leaves begin to limp, stir and quickly remove them from the pan. Dump it over into the reserved pan with the BEP.
- Continue to wilt the remaining spinach until it is all cooked (remember to season).
- Now, you can gently combine all the cooked components.
- Add more spices if needed and reheat desired portions as needed.

Note: Reheat in the microwave or flash sauté it in a medium-heated skillet before serving. Do not hold it hot using a chafing pan and sterno cans. The spinach will turn brownish and not remain green.

Personal Chef Plating: Featuring Cilantro Lime Chicken with Fried Plantains & Seasoned Black Beans + Cajun Seared Fish with BEP Medley

Traditional Plating (An Example Of Seared Fish- Not The Dish Described/ Seared Fish with Roasted Veggies)

Cajun Seared Fish with Herbal purée & BEP Medley

Cajun Seared Fish with Herbal Purée

Yields: about 4-8 portions (depending on portion sizes)

Herbal Purée

- ½ cup fresh herbs (basil, parsley, oregano & or cilantro)
- ¼ cup or so of olive oil (EVOO)
- ¼ cup or so of water, cream or broth
- 2 garlic cloves
- 1 tbsp lemon juice (or tt)
- 1 handful of fresh spinach (for a more vibrant green color)
- Spices- pepper flakes, salt, a pinch of sugar & pepper
- Tools- Standing blender or a hand blender

Procedure (the Purée):

- Wash all the herbs
- Add all the components into a blender or Ninja bullet, season to taste & purée
- Taste & adjust the flavors as needed (add a splash of liquid if it is too thick); set aside

Seared Cajun Fish:

- 4-8 pcs fresh fish filets (salmon, trout, or tilapia)
- Olive oil
- 1 cup vegetable stock
- Sugar (about 1 tbsp)
- Spices- Cajun blend, garlic powder, salt, pepper & cayenne (optional).
- Tools- 14" or 16" skillet, a sheet pan, a pastry brush, a fish spatula, spoon, strainer, paper towels- gather about 8 sheets before handling the raw fish, a digital food thermometer, cutting board & chef's knife.

Prep & Procedure (the Fish):

- Prep the seasoning blend and add about 1 tbsp of sugar to 3 tbsp of the Cajun spice blend (taste the Cajun blend 1st & adjust it if needed, ex: add pepper, cayenne, garlic & salt).
- Set aside.

- Rinse the fish in cold lemon water.
- Thoroughly dry the fish on both sides & brush with olive oil.
- Season both sides using the adjusted Cajun blend.
- Remember to thoroughly clean & sanitize the area where the fish was handled & prepared (wash your hands, sink, counter, faucet, tools, etc.).
- Preheat your oven to 170 to 200°F. This will be used to keep the fish warm until it's ready to serve.
- Preheat the large skillet on medium-high heat.
- When hot, add about 2 tbsp of oil & put the fish in the pan, nice side down.
- DO NOT TOUCH IT! Allow the fish to show signs of browning. The edges will start to look golden & the sides of the flesh will look opaque (cook for about 2 minutes).
- Carefully flip the fish to the other side using a fish spatula.
- Allow the fish to cook for another 1 to 3 minutes or until reading an internal temperature of about 138°F to 140°F. Use a digital food thermometer in the thickest part of the flesh to determine this. Note: Since the fish will be kept warm in the oven, I like to remove it from cooking a little shy of 145°F to avoid dryness. The fish will carryover and cook the remainder of the way.
- Place the fish on a sheet pan.
- Repeat this process until all the fish is cooked. Remember not to overcrowd the sauté pan. This will help you to achieve nice browning.
- Deglaze the skillet with about 1 cup of veggie stock or water & scrape up the brown bits using your spatula.
- Pour the liquid into the pan with the fish.
- Place the fish in broth into the low-heat oven to stay warm until you are ready to plate (no more than 10-20 minutes or so).
- Once ready to serve, plate the fish, drizzle with the herbal purée & serve it with the black-eyed pea medley.
- Enjoy

Cajun Butter

Yields: about 16 portions

This condiment is a perfect alternative to top Cajun fish. Or, use it for cooking garlicky sautéed quick greens! Add it to toasted bagels, hot biscuits, or even sweet cornbread (see the sweet southern cornbread recipe).

Ingredients

- 1 lb. unsalted butter (room temperature, soft)
- Zest of 1 lemon
- Pinch of sugar (about ¼ tsp)
- 1 & ½ tbsp Cajun or blackening spice
- Smoked paprika (about ½ tsp)
- ¼ tsp fine salt
- 4-6 cloves finely minced garlic
- 2 tbsp fresh chopped parsley
- Pinch of cayenne to taste (about 1/8 tsp)
- 1 tbsp lemon juice (adjust tt)

Tools Needed:

Cutting board/ chef's knife, micro-plane zester (fine zester), a bowl & rubber spatula/ spoon.

Method & Procedure:

- Combine all ingredients in a medium-sized bowl.
- Stir until thoroughly mixed (FYI, stir slowly to start as the lemon juice will slowly incorporate).
- Taste & adjust the seasonings & acid level to your liking.
- For easy portioning, pre-scoop 1 ounce dollops onto a parchment-lined sheet pan using a 1 oz ice cream scoop. Then, refrigerate the butter scoops until they harden.
- To avoid spoilage, store it in an airtight container in the fridge until ready for use.
- Allow it to sit at room temperature for at least 20 minutes before serving, as the butter will re-harden once chilled. Yet, I advise that you handle the butter scoops while they're cold & position them on a serving dish to avoid messy plating.

For perfect butter coins at a grab: You can also roll the freshly made compound butter into a slender log using plastic wrap. Once the butter log has hardened in the fridge or freezer, it can be sliced into coins when needed. Or, you can even distribute the soft compound butter into silicone molds before hardening (a silicone ice cube tray will do).

Citrus Fish Pouch

Citrus Fish Pouches
(Simple & Seasonal)

Foil or Parchment Fish Pouches

Serves 8

Fish pouch packets are an excellent make-ahead meal to prep for the Feast of Tabernacles! They are easy, nutritious & very versatile. Just assemble the pouches ahead & freeze them. Think of all the extra time you will gain by planning & prepping some of your F.O.T. meals in advance! Shown is one of many flavor combos. I usually make a version of this every year.

Flavor: Citrus, Thyme & Root Veggies

Ingredients:

- 8 filets of skinless flaky fish (trout, tilapia, bass, grouper, salmon, etc.)
- About 4 lemons + 2 oranges (thinly sliced)
- 6 cloves garlic (finely minced)
- 2 lb. parsnips (peeled & ¼ inch sliced)
- 2 lb. baby carrots
- 2 lb. Yukon gold potatoes (will slice in ¼-inch rounds)
- Fresh thyme sprigs (about 8 sprigs)
- Fruity white wine (chardonnay or pinot grigio)
- 1 stick of butter (sliced)
- Seasonings- salt, pepper, garlic powder (to taste)

Tools- aluminum foil, a cutting board, a knife, a large pot, a veggie peeler, a sheet pan & large zip lock bags

Prep & Procedure:

- Wash the veggies.
- Bring a large pot of water to a boil & add a pinch of sea salt.
- Boil the potatoes whole until about halfway done (parboil).
- Remove them from the water & allow the potatoes to cool.
- Once cooled, slice the potatoes into about ¼-inch rounds.

- Also, quickly boil the baby carrots until about halfway done.
- Season lightly, cool & set aside.
- Peel & slice the parsnips into about ¼-inch rounds.
- Before handling the fish, tear or cut 8 pieces of foil at least double the size of the fish fillets.
- Season both sides of the fish with salt, pepper, & garlic powder.

Assembly:
- Using a large or long surface, line up all the foil sheets (side by side).
- Start building on one-half of the foil sheets leaving about 2 inches from the edge. Equally distribute the potato slices onto each sheet.
- Season the tops of each potato mound with salt, pepper & garlic powder.
- Place a seasoned fish filet on top of each potato mound.
- Add the baby carrots on one side & then place the parsnip slices on top of the carrots.
- Remember to repeat this for each foil sheet.
- Place a few citrus slices on the opposite side of the fish filet of each pouch.
- Put 1 or 2 sprigs of thyme in the center of each fish.
- Carefully drizzle about 2 tbsps. of white wine over each fillet. Note: The use of frozen filets will solidify the liquids added to the pouch. Making assembly an easier, less messy task!
- Now, place a few butter pads on each fillet.

Closing the Pouch: Let's seal them up
- Fold over the opposite half of the foil sheet for each pouch.
- Roll in and crimp the edges tightly. Do this by folding & pinching the foil edges inward to create a tight seal. This would be like sealing a calzone. Proper closure will allow the fish pouch to steam while cooking & not lose liquid which could cause uneven cooking and or dry fish.
- Freeze the pouches in a single layer on a sheet pan.
- Once frozen, place the prepared fish packets into a large zip lock bag to preserve freshness.

- Label, date & freeze them until you are ready for travel. Store them in a cooler on dry ice during your commute.
- Once at your campsite, prepare the grill & place the desired quantity of fish pouches onto the grill. During cooking, they should begin to balloon on top. This is a great sign that the fish is steaming properly. Cook for 12-20 minutes, depending on if the fish is still frozen. It should reach an internal temperature of 145°F.
- Allow it to cool slightly & break open the center of the pouch to enjoy.

Other flavor combinations are endless, but here are a few: fish with roasted vegetables & herbs, fish with garlicky green beans & mushrooms, curry-spiced fish with potatoes, tomato & garbanzos).

Chef's Tip: *This dish works perfectly with quality unbreaded frozen fish fillets.* You can also cook them right away by baking them on a sheet pan directly in the oven. In this case, the fish pouches would not need to be frozen; just bake & enjoy!

Another Fish Pouch Variation

More Fish Pouch Variations

Featuring Lemon, Root Veggies & Mushrooms

Featuring Lemon, Green Beams & Peppers

Chicken Cobb Salad

Yields: about 8 portions

Tools Needed:

A grater or spiralizer, knife & cutting boards, zip bag, tongs, several small serving bowls for toppings & the sauce, a large serving bowl for the lettuce, a large oven safe skillet, spoons for mixing, a mason jar for the dressing

The Chicken

Ingredients:

- 3 chicken breasts (boneless & skinless)
- 3 garlic cloves
- extra virgin olive oil (as needed)
- About 2 tbsp chopped herbs (oregano, basil, dill & parsley)
- 1 lemon (zest & juice)
- Spices (season to taste- I used about ½ tsp of each) Italian seasoning, crushed red pepper flakes, black pepper, granulated garlic & sea salt

Prep & Cook the Chicken:

- Zest the lemon & save the zest for later. Juice the lemon, reserving 1 tbsp of juice for the marinade. Add the remaining juice to a bowl or a cleaned kitchen sink filled halfway with cold water
- Clean the chicken breast in cold water & lemon juice. Remove any cartilage, bone or noticeable vein spots
- If the chicken breasts are large, pat them dry with paper towels before completing the next step. Then, split them in half by cutting the large chicken breasts horizontally at the center. This will promote a shorter & more even cook time.
- Remember to thoroughly wash your hands & work surfaces afterwards
- Season both sides of the chicken with the spices mentioned above. Use a pair of tongs to reduce cross-contamination

- In a large zip bag, add about 3 tbsp of EVOO, half of the lemon zest, a tbsp of lemon juice & half of the chopped herbs
- Allow the chicken to marinated for at least 1 hour or overnight
- Once it's time to cook the chicken, make sure to remove it from the zip bag to a paper towel lined sheet pan or plate. Pat both sides of the chicken dry. Remember, that dry protein allows for browning
- Heat a large oven safe skillet on a medium flame
- Once the pan is hot, add a few drizzles of oil. Brown the chicken. Before turning it, you will notice that the edges of the breast will begin to turn white as the center remains pink. Once the brim of the chicken becomes golden, it's safe to take a peek without risking sticking. If it is golden, flip the chicken over. Add about ½ cup of chicken or veggie broth to the pan
- Now, place the oven safe pan into an oven preheated to 350°F. Bake for about 10 minutes or until the thickest part of each breast reaches 165°F
- When the chicken is fully cooked, allow it to rest for at least 3 minutes before slicing or dicing. This will help the chicken to remain juicy.
- Toss the diced chicken with the remaining chopped herbs, a splash of broth & a drizzle of EVOO. Taste it & add more spices if needed

The Dressing (Easy Lemon Vinaigrette)

Ingredients:

- 1 garlic clove (finely minced)
- About ½ cup extra virgin olive oil (or more)
- 1 tbsp chopped herbs (from those already chopped)
- The remaining lemon zest + the juice of one lemon
- 1 to 2 tbsp of raw honey
- 1 tsp course mustard (or mustard of choice)
- Spices (season to taste) with crushed red pepper flakes, cracked black pepper, granulated garlic & sea salt

Assemble & Shake the Dressing:

Add all of the following ingredients into a mason jar:

- Finely mince the garlic or grate it with a micro-plane
- squeeze the lemon juice of one whole lemon + the remaining lemon zest from prepping the chicken
- Add the EVOO (use a quality olive oil)
- Add the mustard, the honey & add the lid onto the jar. Shake until it has emulsified (comes together)
- Add a little of the seasonings at a time. Stir it around, taste it & adjust it to your liking
- Add more lemon juice if needed
- Bump up the flavor & add any leftover fresh herbs prepped earlier for the chicken. This is optional but would be a complimentary addition! Note that over time, the fresh herbs will lose their vibrant green color as a reaction to the acidic lemon juice. No worries, it will still taste fine.

The Toppings & Set Up

Ingredients:

- 1 zucchini (cut as desired thinly or use the spiralizer)
- Sliced red onions (about ½ of an onion)
- 1 red bell pepper, julienned (any sweet pepper color will do)
- ¼ cup sliced green or kalamata olives
- 1 lb tub of salad greens (spring, baby arugula or spinach, etc)
- ½ of a 10 oz bag of shredded or matchstick cut carrots
- 6 hard-boiled eggs
- 1 pk of turkey bacon (cook crisp & chop)
- 1 pk cherry tomatoes (10 oz)

Procedure:

- Rinse, dry & prep all the veggies as mentioned above
- Put all the sliced veggies into individual small serving bowls.

- Put the salad greens of your choice in a large serving bowl
- This Cobb salad is a great option for a scrumptious cold meal buffet. Or, if it's preferred, you can create composed salad plates for your guests instead.
- Boil, cool & chop up the whole eggs. Season lightly with salt & pepper (For in-depth instructions, see the perfectly boiled eggs recipe in the Essentials & Tips section).
- Time to prepare the turkey bacon bits. If the turkey bacon is damp, pat it dry first. Bake the meat in an oven preheated to 400°F with a drizzle of oil. Be sure to crisp both sides. Or sauté it in a large skillet on the stovetop using medium high heat & a bit of oil. Cook the strips on both sides until they begin to foam & crisp up. Drain off the excess oil on paper towels & chop. Put the crispy turkey bacon pieces in a small serving bowl & set it aside until later.
- Now, it's time to beautify your table & create the buffet
- Don't forget to place serving utensils, serving bowls, or plates & present the homemade dressing.
- By the way, you can use up any leftovers, in an omelet, in soup, or even a veggie potato hash! Although, I would exclude the carrots from the omelet.

Chef's tip: This meal would be a great option to have to go into the Sabbath on Friday night! *Or, if there is turkey bacon leftover from Sabbath breakfast; chop it up & eliminate one step from this recipe to create an easy Sunday dinner. Bon appetite!*

Chicken Cobb Salad

Cobb Salad Toppings

Cous Cous Salad

Chicken Gyros with Fresh Tzatziki *Served with Cous Cous Salad*

Yields: about 6 portions (depending on portion sizes)

Tt = to taste

Tbsp = tablespoon

EVOO = extra virgin olive oil

M= for the marinade

The Tzatziki Sauce/Spread

You can make this dish as a cold Sabbath sandwich or serve it while the chicken is hot on another day. Keep it fresh & add the cold toppings to each gyro before serving. Also, the sauce can be stabilized by adding a bit of mayo. This is a great alternative if you plan to offer the gyros as a cold meal option.

Needed Tools: chef's knife, cutting board, individual serving bowls or family-style platter & bowl, fine zester (micro-plane), basic grater, 1 large zip bag, 3-5 smaller prep bowls, 2 medium bowls to assemble the salad & sauce, plastic wrap, 2 tongs, 1-2 rubber spatulas, 1 heat-safe spoon, 1 oven safe skillet, sandwich frills (optional) & a digital meat thermometer

Seasoning Spice Mix- 1 tbsp each of granulated garlic, onion powder, poultry seasoning, Italian blend; 1 tsp black pepper & salt to taste (about ½ tbsp); combine & store in a small container with a lid (label & date any excess, it can be used for a later date)

Our Fresh Herb Mix- 2 tbsp each of chopped dill, flat-leaf parsley, thyme, oregano & rosemary (This can be simplified to only the dill, parsley & oregano.). We will utilize this mix throughout the recipe. While chopping, set aside an additional tbsp of dill to add to the tzatziki.

Making the Tzatziki

Ingredients:

- 1 tbsp fresh dill (chopped)
- 1 tbsp fresh herb mix
- ½ cup plain Greek yogurt (substitute- sour cream)
- 2 tbsp mayo
- Zest & juice of ½ a lemon

- 1 clove of garlic (finely minced)
- ½ tsp spice mix
- ¼ of an English cucumber (grated & squeezed of all moisture)
- 1 tbsp red onion (finely diced)
- Salt & cracked black (tt)

Method: To make the tzatziki, combine all ingredients in a medium-sized bowl and mix thoroughly. Taste & adjust the seasonings to your liking. Wrap & refrigerate until sandwich assembly.

Chicken Gyro Prep

Chef's Tip: Prepare enough chicken for 2 meals (instead of 3, make 6). Often, the meat is the hardest & most costly part of a meal to deal with. This will give you a great head start for Sunday dinner. You can even freeze it to use for the following Sabbath!!!

Chicken Ingredients: m= for the marinade

- 3 boneless/ skinless chicken breast
- About 2 tbsp seasoning spice mix, 2 tsp in the marinade (see page 115)
- Juice & zest of half a lemon, m.
- 1 tbsp of our fresh herb mix
- 2 sprigs each of thyme, rosemary & oregano, m. (if available after making the herb mix, optional)
- ¼ cup white wine, m. (optional)
- Pinch of red pepper flakes, m.
- 3 cloves garlic, m. (finely minced)
- ¼ cup EVOO (1/2 in marinade, ½ for garnish)
- Additional olive oil for cooking (about 3 tbsp; canola or regular olive oil)
- 2 cups chicken stock (not for the marinade)
- None stick pan spray (optional)

Condiment Ingredients:

- 2 Roma tomatoes (seeded, dried & julienned)
- ¼ of an English cucumber (thinly sliced)
- ¼ of a red onion (thinly sliced)
- Leaf lettuce (washed, spun dry & halved)
- Feta cheese (optional)
- Olives of choice (kalamata preferred, optional)
- Soft pita bread (no pocket needed)

Method:

Marinate the Chicken. Use the large zip bag to add about 2 tsp of our spice mix & all ingredients for the marinade (except for the spray). Stir it around in the bag. Add the chicken along with the remaining shell of the squeezed lemon. Remove the air from the bag & close it tightly. Rotate it around to ensure that the chicken is well coated. Place the bag on a plate & put it on the lowest shelf in your fridge (away from ready-to-eat foods) to marinate.

Marinate overnight or for at least 1 hour. Be sure to thoroughly clean each area where you worked with the raw chicken with an antibacterial cleaner. Even the sink, faucet & all surface areas to avoid cross-contamination. Thoroughly wash your hands. Ensure that no other items are contaminated with the raw chicken before proceeding to the next step.

Prep the cold toppings. Next, you can utilize this time to get all the condiments together. Make a row of about 3 paper bowls to use for each item. This makes for easy clean-up. You can put the cleaned lettuce in a large zip bag lined with paper towels. Or, you can use pre-washed baby spinach or arugula as your lettuce for less work. Choose what suits your household & needs.

Complete the chicken prep. Remove it from the fridge. Line the plate with paper towels. Remove the chicken & pat it dry. Discard the bag with the marinade & the paper towels. Wash your hands & use antibacterial wipes to clean up the area where you worked with the chicken. Season both sides of the meat generously with the spice mix & a sprinkle of the fresh herb mix, handle with tongs to flip & repeat. You can watch my YouTube channel to see me prepare this recipe in depth. Check out the "how to meal prep for Sabbath" video.

Pre-heat a large oven-safe skillet. Spray lightly with the non-stick spray. Once the pan is hot, add a drizzle of oil & sear the chicken on one side. This will take about one minute. Do not play with it or move it around. It will release from the pan when it is browned. Flip it. No longer use this pair of tongs. When checking the chicken later, use a clean set of tongs.

Deglaze the pan with the wine, about 1 cup of chicken stock & a tbsp or so of lemon juice. Pour the liquid around the chicken, not directly on it. Turn off the heat & bake in a 350°F pre-heated oven for about 10-15 minutes or until fully cooked (165 degrees F). Once ready, remove the chicken from the pan onto a clean plate or dish & allow it to fully cool. Pour about ¼ cup of stock over it. Remove the flavor from the bottom of the skillet by deglazing with about ½ cup of stock. Complete the deglazing by scrapping up the brown bits.

Once cooled, add the chicken to a zip bag & pour over the broth from both the deglazed pan & the plate. Close the bag & refrigerate. This will allow the juices to redistribute into the chicken as it gets cold. Chill for at least 2 hours. However, this process can be done in half the time using the freezer. It must be at room temperature before refrigerating or freezing to avoid spoilage or overheating in the fridge/ freezer.

After properly chilling the chicken, slice it thinly against the meat grain. Dress it with a few spoonfuls of the broth, a drizzle of olive oil, and a few pinches of our spice mix, Finally, sprinkle the chicken with more of the chopped herbs. Set aside or refrigerate until assembly.

Gyro Assembly

Begin with washed hands & a cleaned/ sanitized work surface. Gather all components from the fridge, the feta, olives, & pita—Line the length of the assembly workspace with plastic wrap or foil. Behind the workspace, line up the bowls of cold toppings & other items. Working assembly-line style is the fastest.

Place all pitas bottom side up. Systematically add all components to one side, beginning with the tzatziki sauce (about 1 tbsp). Next, add the chicken, cucumber, tomato, red onion & so on. The last item to add is the lettuce. Close it by folding over the lettuce side on top of the other ingredients. Pick it closed with a sandwich frill pick (I love these). Platter them or individually wrap them for the next day. This is a nice switch-up from the typical cold sandwich meal. It's an awesome Sabbath treat made with love!

Cous Cous Salad

Ingredients:

- About 2 cups of cooked pearl cous cous
- 1 Roma tomato (seeded & diced)
- ¼ of an English cucumber (diced)
- ¼ of a red onion (finely chopped)
- 1 standard can of garbanzo beans (rinsed & drained)
- ¼ to ½ cup EVOO
- 2 tbsp fresh herb blend
- 1 tbsp spice mix
- Salt & pepper (tt)
- Juice & zest of ½ lemon
- Feta cheese (optional)
- Olives of choice (kalamata preferred, optional)
- 1 small zucchini (washed & small diced, optional)
- Baby spinach or arugula (washed & spun dry)

Cous Cous Salad Assembly

- Follow the directions on the packaging to cook the cous cous properly. It is basically small beads of pasta. Cook it slightly under, which is considered al dente "to the tooth." This will prevent it from becoming mushy as it cools.
- Rinse the pasta with cool water to help stop the cooking.
- Drain & add it to a medium-sized mixing bowl.
- Chop the spinach. Add in all the prepped veggies, add the zest & juice of half a lemon.
- Add the olive oil, herbs & seasonings.
- Taste & adjust it to your liking.
- Finish it with the feta & olives.
- Garnish with the remaining fresh herbs. If there are any left.

Keep in mind that this side is excellent to assemble after making the gyros! This recipe uses many of the same ingredients included for the gyro veggie prep. You can reduce your workload by using up the leftover toppings.

Chicken & Fish Piccata Personal Chef Style

Piccata

Piccata with Parmesan Sweet Pea Mash- PC Plating

Family Buffet Style- Piccata Served with Parmesan Sweet Pea Mash

Chicken Piccata *with lemon & capers*

Served with a parmesan sweet pea mash

Ingredients:

- 3-6 boneless, skinless chicken breasts
- 1 box chicken stock
- 2 lemons
- 2 tbsp capers
- 4-6 cloves garlic (½ minced, ½ sliced)
- 3-6 lbs. potatoes (russet, Yukon or red)
- 1 bag frozen sweet peas
- 2-4 oz parmesan (grated or shaved)
- 1 qt heavy cream or half & half
- white wine (fruity chardonnay or pinot grigio)
- up to 1 stick butter (as needed)
- up to ½ cup olive or canola oil
- AP flour (as needed)
- ½ onion or 1 shallot
- parsley (to garnish)

Seasonings- salt, pepper, garlic, lemon zest, a pinch of red pepper flakes (optional)

Tools: Chef's knife & cutting board, 2 pairs of tongs, a sheet pan, a large container or zip bag to dredge, veggie peeler, cheese grater (if the parm isn't bought grated), hand mixer or a sturdy whisk, a large pot, a large skillet, a mallet or something for pounding, plastic wrap, a blender or bullet, a spoon or rubber spatula, a wine opener & a strainer

Prep to Cook Next Day: Peel the potatoes & store in cold water; mince the garlic; thaw the peas; clean the chicken ahead (rinse it in lemon water & remove unwanted fat & gristle, slice it in half horizontally to make cutlets); mise en place before beginning the final cook

Method & Procedure (Starting the Chicken & the Parmesan Sweet Pea Mash):

- Peel & boil the potatoes. Tender skin potato varieties (like Yukon) can be left unpeeled if you prefer.
- Clean & fabricate the chicken (trim off the fat & gristle).
- Slice the chicken horizontally to speed up cooking time & to stretch out the meat.
- Pound the chicken into an even layer (before pounding, wedge it between plastic or in a large zip bag to prevent tears).
- Season both sides of the poultry with salt, pepper, garlic & lemon zest.
- Lightly dust the chicken in flour, pat off the excess.
- Set it aside & prepare to pan fry.
- Begin to shallow fry the chicken. Depending on the quantity, this may require batch cooking.
- While the chicken cooks, drain the potatoes.
- Add the potatoes back into the pot, whip them together using the hand mixer or whisk.
- Purée about 1 cup of the peas with the minced garlic in the blender with a bit of stock or cream.
- Add the pea purée & a bit of the whole peas to the whipped potatoes.
- Remember to check on the chicken & continue to cook it in stages. Cook the cutlets until golden on both sides.
- Return to the potatoes.
- Add cream or half -n- half until it is smooth.
- Add butter to taste.
- Once the mash is at your preferred consistency, add the parmesan.
- Season the mash to taste with salt, pepper & granulated garlic.
- Turn the mash pot on low until it's time to serve.
- Place the browned chicken aside. It will be added to the sauce later to simmer.

The Sauce & Finishing Up:

- Pour off the excess oil from the chicken skillet.

- Wipe out the excess browned bits.

- Lightly sauté the onions or shallots, sliced garlic & capers until translucent.

- Deglaze the pan with white wine (about 1 cup).

- Cook until it reduces in half & add about ½ box of chicken stock (2 cups or so).

- Season to taste & add a touch of butter. You may need to slightly thicken the sauce with a little cornstarch slurry. It should only coat the back of a spoon thinly.

- Add the browned chicken to the sauce to reheat & simmer. Allow it to cook until aromatic & hot.

- Serve the chicken piccata in a bit of the pan sauce & with the parmesan sweet pea mash.

- Garnish with fresh lemon zest, cracked pepper, shaved parmesan & fresh chopped parsley.

Easy Chicken & Split Pea Soup

Ingredients:

- 2 qts. chicken stock
- ½ tbsp rosemary (chopped)
- ½ tbsp oregano (chopped)
- 1 lb. chicken thighs (boneless/ skinless)
- 1 cup frozen spinach (or chopped kale)
- 2 medium onions (diced)
- 2-3 tbsp quick roux
- 1 cup green bell pepper (diced)
- 4 bay leaves
- 2-4 cups tap water
- 1 pk plain gnocchi
- 4 sprigs fresh thyme (remove the leaves & chop)
- 6 cloves garlic (minced)
- 3 medium carrots (peeled & sliced)
- 3 stalks celery (diced)
- 1 (16 oz) bag of dried split peas
- 1 tbsp EVOO
- 1 large yellow squash (diced)

Spices (tt): granulated garlic, onion powder, s & p, 2 tbsp fresh chopped herbs (parsley, oregano, rosemary & thyme)

Method & Procedure:

The Split Peas

- Check the dried split peas for small pebbles, discard if any and rinse.
- Add the split peas into a medium sized pot; add about 3 cups of stock.

- To the pot, add half of the minced garlic, 2 bay leaves & ½ tsp each of s & p, granulated garlic & onion powder.
- Bring it to a rapid boil. Boil for 5 minutes.
- Lower to a simmer & allow it to cook gently for about 15-20 minutes.
- Stir occasionally and add about ½ cup of water at a time if the liquid cooks out during this period.
- After 15-20 minutes, turn off the heat & cover the pot of split peas with the lid, Set it aside until later. This will allow them to steam & gently finish cooking without becoming excessively mushy.

The Soup

- On a sheet pan, add your cleaned chicken.
- Season both sides with salt, pepper, granulated garlic & about a tsp of the chopped herbs.
- Place the sheet pan on a middle rack in an oven preheated to 375°F. Add about 1 cup of stock to a corner of the pan.
- Bake it for about 20 minutes but do not fully cook it.
- Remove the chicken from the oven when the chicken reads an internal temperature of about 145°F. This will help prevent the meat from becoming dry as it continues to cook in the soup. Note: Dark meat is more forgiving, but this is especially so if using chicken breasts.
- Allow the chicken to cool in the juices. Cut it into medium to large dice. Set aside. Be mindful not to cross-contaminate. Remember, the chicken isn't fully cooked.
- Now, heat a large pot on medium-high heat.
- Add about 1 tbsp of the EVOO & all the minced garlic.
- Lightly brown it & add a pinch of red pepper flakes, stir.
- Quickly add half of the onion, celery & peppers; add all the carrots.
- Stir, then add 1 qt of the chicken stock.
- Stir & allow the soup to simmer for about 30 minutes.
- Add half of the chopped herbs.
- Season the soup with about ½ tsp each of the granulated garlic & onion powders.

- Season to taste with salt & pepper.
- Add the quick roux one tbsp at a time, stirring thoroughly to incorporate.
- Allow the soup to come to a boil after adding the roux. Roux reaches its full thickening ability once it comes to a boil.
- Continue to add the quick roux until it has thickened to your desired consistency (see quick roux in essential recipes). Keep in mind that the split peas will also help to thicken the soup.
- Taste & adjust the seasonings if needed.
- Reduce the heat to a low simmer.
- Add the packaged potato gnocchi and stir.
- Add the partially cooked chicken, the rest of the diced veggies, the yellow squash, the chopped frozen spinach & the cooked split peas with their broth.
- Stir & allow it to simmer for about 15 minutes. Or, until the gnocchi is tender & fully cooked.
- Taste & adjust where needed. If it is under-seasoned, correct it here. If it is too thick, add a little more stock. If it is too thin, add a bit more quick roux. But, remember, when using a roux, it must boil to reach its full thickness.
- All done!
- Serve with warm dinner rolls, a garnish of the remaining chopped herbs & shaved parmesan.

Other Potential Garnishes: shaved parmesan or Italian cheeses, a dollop of crème fresh, chopped herbs, crispy turkey bacon bits, chopped chives, quick sautéed veggies or even seared seasoned mushrooms

Note: Make this a vegan dish by eliminating the chicken & substituting the chicken stock with vegetable stock.

Fried Rice

129

Fried Rice Your Way...

The key to great fried rice at home lies in 2 things: cold rice & organization. You must have everything prepped ahead & ready to go before starting "mise en place."

Stir-frying is a quick cooking method & a great way to prepare a fast, nutritious dinner. Each item will be cooked in the same pan. As an item finishes cooking, scrape it onto a clean sheet pan. Then, continue to cook each item as instructed.

Want a healthier alternative? Substitute the rice for an ancient grain or riced cauliflower. Remember, the best part of making your own dishes is the ability to customize! Let's get started.

The Foundation Ingredients:
- Specific tools- wok or large skillet, heat safe spoon, sheet pan, chef's knife/ cutting board
- 2-6 tbsp canola, peanut or olive oil as needed
- 4 to 6 cups of cold rice
- 3 whole eggs (beat with 1 tbsp water)
- 1 lb. chicken- boneless/ skinless (diced)
- 1 onion (diced)
- 1 tbsp minced ginger
- 2 to 4 tbsp sesame oil
- 3 cloves garlic (minced)
- Spices to taste: (about 2 tbsp Asian spice mix, a pinch of pepper flakes, s & p tt)
- 2 tbsp cilantro (chopped) or sliced scallions for garnish

The Veggies: it's up to you
- 1 zucchini (diced)
- ½ bag of frozen peas & carrots
- Napa cabbage (shredded, washed & dried)

The Sauce: mix all the sauce ingredients in a small bowl, set aside

- ¼ cup soy sauce + 2 tbsp of sesame oil (toasted is better)
- ¼ cup chicken stock
- ¼ tsp sugar
- ¼ tsp rice wine vinegar or lime juice
- ½ tsp corn starch
- Pinch of crushed red pepper flakes
- 1 tsp each of minced garlic & fresh ginger

Prep & Method:

- Season the raw, diced chicken with about 1 tsp of the Asian blend.
- Heat the wok or large skillet on high and add about 1 tbsp canola oil.
- Season the beaten eggs with a pinch of s & p, scramble them & set them aside on the sheet pan.
- Add about 1 tsp oil.
- Quickly stir fry the chicken until browned & fully cooked; remove from the pan by adding it to a new pile on the same sheet pan as the eggs.
- Add oil, quickly stir-fry the zucchini, season with a little of the Asian spice mix (it should still be undercooked, browned a bit & bright green), and add to the sheet pan.
- Add oil, add the cabbage & season. Cook quickly; set aside.
- Add oil, add the remaining fresh ginger & garlic, and stir (careful not to burn it).
- Quickly add the cold rice, stir & season with about 1 tsp of the spice mix & sesame oil tt.
- Stir fry the rice until it is completely hot throughout.
- Add all the ingredients from the sheet pan, add the peas & carrots, add most of the sauce & all if needed; mix thoroughly.
- Turn off the heat, adjust spices if needed & garnish with the fresh herbs & toasted sesame seeds (optional).

What a great way to utilize leftover cold rice! Don't have any to start, no problem. Just cook & chill your rice the day before. For one-on-one instructions, watch my YouTube channel to see me prepare this recipe. Check out the "how to make veggie loaded fried rice" video.

Fried Green Tomatoes

Fried Green Tomatoes

Serves: about 10

Ingredients

-4 large green tomatoes

-½ cup milk

-1 tbsp sugar

-2 eggs

-1 cup AP flour

-¼ cup corn starch

-hot sauce (a few shakes)

-½ cup butter cracker crumbs (like crushed Ritz)

-1 cup cornmeal

-1 qt canola or veggie oil (2+ cups needed for frying)

- Spices to taste (salt, pepper, paprika, optional- granulated garlic, cracked pepper & smoked sea salt)

Items Needed:

- Cutting board/ sharp chef's knife
- 3 medium containers (breading station)
- Whisk or fork/ tongs/ mesh spoon
- Large skillet or 4 qt pot (for frying)
- Draining rack or paper towels/ sheet pan/ parchment or foil

Prep & Procedure

Build the Breading Station

- Note that this recipe uses the 3-step breading process. Try to use one hand to dredge & use tongs in place of the other. It's vital to keep one clean hand.

- In one of the medium containers, combine the flour & cornstarch (season with salt, pepper & a pinch of garlic).
- In the 2nd container, combine the corn meal & cracker crumbs (season with salt, pepper & paprika).
- In the 3rd container, combine the eggs, milk & sugar, and whisk= egg wash (season with salt, pepper, hot sauce & a pinch of granulated garlic).

Prep & Coat the Tomatoes

- Wash, core & cut the tomatoes into about ¼" to ½" thick slices.
- Season well with salt & pepper. To kick up the flavor, season them with the Cajun spice mix.
- Line a sheet pan with foil or parchment for easy cleanup.
- Create an assembly line starting with the seasoned tomatoes, dipping them in the flour mix, egg wash & then the corn meal mix.
- Place the foil or parchment-lined sheet pan at the end. This will be a place to land the breaded tomatoes.
- The breading process will likely be done in a few batches of 4-6 slices at a time.
- Start by lightly coating the tomatoes in the flour and shake off excess flour.
- Then dip them in the egg wash, coating each side.
- Finally, dip them in the corn meal mix. Be sure to try to coat both sides & the edges if possible.
- Rest the finished breaded tomatoes on the lined sheet pan.
- Continue this process until all the tomatoes are breaded. Be sure that they are in one single layer.
- Should you run out of room, simply wash up & cover the 1st layer of prepared tomatoes with another piece of foil or parchment, then continue until done.
- For the best results, allow the tomatoes to be set up in the fridge (about 30 minutes) or freezer (about 10 minutes) to help ensure that the breading remains intact.

Let's Fry Em...

- Preheat the frying oil in a large skillet or 4 qt pot on med heat while you tidy up the mess. You should have at least a half inch of oil and room for expansion (see Chapter 8 for frying tips).
- Set up a draining station with a sheet pan, draining rack & tongs, or spider (large mesh slotted spoon) for frying. The draining rack is not necessary but will help keep the tomatoes crisp.
- Once the oil is hot, fry about 4-5 slices of the tomatoes at a time. Do not overcrowd the pan, as this will cause them to be soggy & not allow for proper frying. Note that they should not touch.
- Allow them to get browned on each side. Drain on the rack or paper towels & finish with a touch of smoked salt & cracked pepper fresh out of the hot oil. Enjoy!

For visual instructions, check out my "how to make southern fried green tomatoes" video on YouTube.

Garnish & Serving Possibilities

- Add a crunchy component & serve them with goat cheese & a sweet beet salad.
- Eat open-faced atop toasted oat bread with seasoned avocado slices & fresh micro greens.
- Drizzle with balsamic reduction & add goat cheese crumbles & fresh cracked pepper
- Eat with a sweet & spicy pineapple compote & top with micro cilantro for that sweet, tangy, crunchy & spicy bite.
- Enjoy as a side with the Cajun seared fish & black-eyed pea medley.
- Keep it simple & enjoy it with some good old-fashioned fresh garlic herb aioli.

Garlicky Sautéed Quick Greens

Close up

Garlicky Sautéed Quick Greens

Serving: About 6

This recipe concept can be applied to any quick-cooking green. Baby or regular spinach, baby kale, arugula, bok choy & swiss chard are some good quick cooking options for dark leafy greens. They are packed full of nutrients & cancer-fighting compounds. A quick sauté in EVOO or butter with a bit of seasoning is all they need!

Ingredients:

- 2.5 lb. tender greens of choice (ex: swiss chard, arugula, spinach, baby kale)
- 4 garlic cloves (minced or sliced)
- 2 tbsp EVOO
- 1 tbsp butter (optional)

Spices- granulated garlic, onion powder, a pinch of pepper flakes, sea salt & black pepper or the Judah blend (tt)

Tools- a cutting board, a chef's knife, a large skillet (12"-14"), a colander & a salad spinner

Prep & Procedure:

- Wash, drain & spin the excess water from the greens of choice.
- Heat the skillet on medium-high heat. Note: If you use minced garlic, lower the heat. This helps to avoid burnt bitter garlic as it is smaller & will cook faster. Also, should you choose swiss chard, chop the leaves & lower stems separately. The stems will need a few minutes more to cook than the leaves. So, begin the sauté process by cooking the stems for about 5 minutes prior to wilting the leafy greens.
- Add the EVOO & the garlic, stirring continuously to avoid burning the garlic
- Add the butter & pepper flakes, stir
- Immediately add the greens gradually while stirring
- Continue to do so until all have been added to the pan
- Season to taste with the spices above. Cook until wilted, tender to the tooth & still vibrant in color.
- Serve as a quick healthy green alongside your favorite dish!
- Get creative & try adding in different components like (dried cranberries, pine nuts, roasted red bell peppers, onions, or even finish with a few crumbles of feta to jazz it up.

Garlic & Herb Hummus

Hummus Your Way…

Servings: About 6-8

Hummus is very versatile and nutritious. Here is a basic recipe. But, the possibilities are endless. You could vary the type of bean as well as some of the other components added. The basic must-haves for hummus include beans, oil, a fresh element (like herbs), acid (citrus or vinegar), garlic, tahini paste & seasonings. You could easily make a spicy black bean hummus by using lime as the acid, adding cilantro as the herb & even adding a little chipotle in adobo for that smoky, spicy element.

Garlic & Herb

Ingredients:

- 1 ea 15.5 oz can garbanzo beans
- 2 cloves garlic (minced)
- 1 tbsp lemon juice
- 1 tbsp tahini paste or ½ tsp sesame oil)
- ¼ cup water
- ¼ to ½ cup extra virgin olive oil

Spices- sea salt, pepper, garlic powder, cumin & paprika (to taste)

Tools- a blender, a cutting board, a knife, a strainer & an airtight container for storage

Prep & Procedure:

- Drain & rinse the beans.
- Add all the ingredients except the spices & only ¼ cup olive oil at a time into a blender.
- Blend until smooth.
- Gradually add the remaining olive oil until the hummus is your desired texture. To reduce the amount of oil used, a little water can be added (1/8 to ¼ cup).
- Season to taste with the spices (add about ¼ tsp each of all except the salt, blend again & add the desired amount of salt.
- Adjust the flavor further if needed (if you like it garlicky, add more; if you like more lemon essence, add a little lemon zest or more lemon juice; for more heat or spice, add a pinch of pepper flakes or cracked black pepper).

- Serve it with fresh-cut veggies (crudité), pita chips, pretzels, or even corn chips.

It's up to you… Have fun & get creative!

Chef's Tip: All out of tahini paste? No problem! Did you know that tahini is actually toasted sesame seed paste? With that said, you can easily substitute the tahini with a bit of toasted sesame seed oil. Just know that the amount needed will be much less. So, start with using ½ tsp at a time until the flavor of the hummus suites your palate. Enjoy!

Other potential flavor combinations:
Southwestern chipotle, roasted veggie, red pepper & herb, carrot & fennel, etc.

Simple Sautéed Asparagus

Simple Green Beans

Simple Sautéed Asparagus or Green Beans

Yields: about 6 portions

Ingredients

- A 2½ pound bunch of asparagus spears
- 4-6 garlic cloves
- 1 sliced shallot or 1 small sliced red onion (optional)
- 2-3 tbsp olive oil
- 1 tbsp unsalted butter (optional)
- Water (as needed)

Spices- Season to taste with salt, pepper, granulated garlic & a pinch of crushed red pepper flakes

Tools Needed- a chef's knife & cutting board, a large 12" to 14" skillet, a large rubber spatula or wooden spoon, a large 4-6 qt pot (for blanching), a large bowl (for shocking), a strainer or colander & about 2 cups of ice

Method & Procedure: Blanch & Prep

- Let's begin with the blanching process.
- Fill the large pot with water & bring it to a rolling boil.
- In the meantime, you can prep the asparagus & get your ice water bowl ready.
- Rinse the asparagus in cold water.
- Trim the spears- Trim off about 1 ½ inches of the spears from the bottom. This can be done easily by keeping the rubber band on them before cutting. If you feel this may be removing too much, simply remove one spear from the bundle. Gently bend it where it naturally snaps. Now, you can use this spear as a guide to cut the others. Why are we cutting them? Well, the ends of the asparagus spears are quite stringy, woody & unpleasant to eat. You could save them for a puréed asparagus soup! Just put the clean ends in a zip bag, then label & freeze them for your convenience.
- Fill the large bowl with ice & water.
- Slice or mince the fresh garlic & set it aside.
- Peel & slice the shallot into about ¼-inch rings & set aside.

Time To Blanch, Shock & Sauté.

- By now, the water should be boiling.
- Place the cleaned & trimmed asparagus spears into the boiling water.
- Allow them to remain in hot water only until they become bright, vivid green. This may take about 30 to 40 seconds.
- Strain the asparagus over the sink in the colander
- Shock It.
- Immediately add the blanched asparagus to the ice water bath. This process is called shocking. It will instantly stop the cooking & lock in that bright green color.
- Once the asparagus is cold, return it to the strainer & set it aside.
- This entire process sounds long-winded but will only take about 10 minutes.

Time to Sauté.

- Preheat your large skillet over medium-high heat.
- Once hot, add a few drizzles of olive oil & the blanched asparagus.
- Season it to taste with salt, pepper, granulated garlic & a pinch of crushed red pepper flakes.
- Sauté it on high heat for about one minute.
- Add the sliced garlic, shallots & another little drizzle of oil. Lower the temperature slightly
- Gently move the asparagus around in the pan until the garlic begins to become fragrant & golden. If this method is used to prepare haricot vert (a tender French green bean), you may need to add a splash of broth or water after browning the garlic. This will pull up the brown bits & give quick steam to ensure doneness. Finally, finish them with a touch of butter for added richness. Taste & adjust the seasonings if needed.
- Turn off the heat & serve.

This would be a great side to accompany nearly any dish. It's a perfect pair for the brown sugar bourbon hens.

Smoky Garlic & Quinoa Salad

Servings: 8-12

Ingredients:

- 1 can garbanzo beans (drained & rinsed)
- 4 cloves garlic (minced)
- ¼ red onion (finely diced)
- ½ each of red, yellow & green bell pepper (small diced)
- 2 tbsp parsley (chopped)
- 1 zucchini (small diced)
- 1 yellow squash (small diced)
- ½ lemon (zest & juice)
- 2-4 tbsp EVOO
- 2 cups cooked quinoa
- About ½ cup sun dried tomatoes (finely chopped)
- About 1 tsp raw sugar or honey

Tools- a sheet pan, a medium pot with a lid (to cook the quinoa), a cutting board, a chef's knife, a fine zester (micro-plane), a large bowl, a large skillet & a sheet pan

Spices- add about 1 tsp smoked paprika. You'll also need about ½ tsp each of granulated garlic, onion powder, black pepper & cumin; add smoked sea salt to taste

- **Note**: Smoke salt might be found at Whole Foods, Sprouts, Trader Joe's, or even Amazon. If you're unable to get your hands on the smoked sea salt, just use regular sea salt & add a little liquid smoke to taste (to the salad). Careful not to add too much as there may be a prevalent artificial aftertaste. For a more southwestern flare, add 2 to 4 tbsp of finely minced chipotle in adobo.

Prep & Procedure:

- Cook & cool the quinoa in broth (follow the instructions on the box & season it).
- Wash & cut the veggies to the suggested sizes mentioned above & put them in a large bowl.
- Heat a sauté pan on medium heat.
- Add about 1 tbsp EVOO & the garlic.
- Once the garlic begins to get golden, add the garbanzo beans & stir. Lower the heat.
- Add another drizzle of EVOO, the chopped sundried tomatoes & the sugar, and stir.

- Add the spices to the pan to toast and stir continuously.
- The goal is only to cook the spices until they become aromatic & the tomatoes are slightly sticky & caramelized.
- Be careful not to burn the garlic or spices during the toasting period. That should only take about 1 minute.
- Cool the garbanzo bean mixture on a sheet pan.
- Once cooled, add the bean mix to the quinoa.
- Add half of the lemon zest, the lemon juice, all the diced veggies & a few tbsp of EVOO to the bowl.
- Add half of the parsley & mix it up thoroughly.
- Taste & adjust the spices to your liking.
- Pour this summer salad into a serving bowl.
- Garnish the top with a drizzle of good quality EVOO, a sprinkle of smoked paprika & the remaining lemon zest & parsley. Keep it chilled in the fridge until serving time.

This salad is very versatile. It can be served warm, at room temperature, or even cold, as described above.

Spicy Asian Kale – Full Picture

Spicy Asian Kale – Close up

Spicy Asian Kale & Cucumber Salad

Serves 8

Ingredients:

- 3 bunches fresh kale (chopped)
- 1 shallot (sliced)
- 2-4 scallions (chopped)
- 4 cloves garlic (finely minced)
- 1 tsp ginger (finely minced)
- 1 yellow squash (halved & sliced)
- 1 large, sweet bell pepper (seeded & chopped)
- 1 thinly sliced jalapeño
- about ¼ cup cashew or peanut pieces
- 1 large cucumber (halved & sliced)
- *Optional- 4 avocados (halved & sliced before serving)

The Sauce- combine ¼ cup soy or liquid amino, 1/4 cup olive oil, about 3 tbsp sesame oil, ½ tsp lime juice, about ¼ tsp of the spice mix & 1-3 tsp raw honey (adjust it to your liking); set aside

Spices- Use the Oriental Express blend or make a spice mix by combining about ½ tsp of the following: ginger, sesame seeds, coriander, cumin, onion powder, garlic powder; add these to your heat & salt preference (to taste) – sea salt (wait until the end, it may not be needed), white pepper & a dry sriracha spice

Tools- a cutting board, a knife, a large bowl, a small bowl, a whisk, a salad spinner & tongs to toss

Prep & Procedure:

- Wash all of the veggies. Spin the kale dry.
- Chop or cut as mentioned on the ingredient list.
- Combine all the chopped components in a large bowl. This includes the nuts
- Toss the ingredients with about half of the dressing. (The extra sauce is nice to drizzle on the avocado slices, which should be added on top of individual portions once the salad is done.)

- Season to taste with the spice mix (reserve the excess in a jar & label "Asian Blend or Oriental Express"). It can be used for other recipes in the future.
- To serve a portion, present it in a bowl, add a sliced avocado half & drizzle it with a little of the extra sauce.
- Garnish with a sprinkle of toasted sesame seeds & chopped green onion or cilantro.

Sweet Southern Cornbread

Cornbread – Close Up

Southern Sweet Cornbread

Serving: 12 wedges

Ingredients:

- 1 ½ yellow cornmeal
- 1 cup & 1 tbsp AP flour
- 1 tbsp & ½ tsp baking powder
- ¼ cup raw sugar (use up to ½ cup for sweeter bread)
- 1 tsp raw honey (or a squirt)
- 1 tsp heavy cream (a splash or so)
- 1 ¼ cup milk
- 1/3 cup vegetable oil
- A pinch of sea salt
- 2 large eggs (room temp)
- 2 tbsp butter (to melt in the skillet)

Procedure:

- Preheat the oven to 350°F.
- Combine all the dry ingredients, whisk well to break up any lumps.
- Add all the wet ingredients, including the eggs into the dry mix.
- Mix well.
- Allow the batter to rest for about 3-5 minutes.
- While this is taking place, put the butter in an 8"- cast iron skillet.
- Place the skillet with the butter into the preheated oven.
- Allow the butter to melt.
- Once melted, carefully get the skillet out of the oven.
- Stir the cornbread batter once more, then add it to the hot skillet.
- Lightly sprinkle about 1 tsp of sugar all over the top. Add more for a sweeter crusty top
- Place the cornbread batter-filled skillet back into the oven to bake.
- This usually takes 18 to 22 minutes, depending on your oven.
- Set a timer for 18 minutes & then check it by poking the center with a toothpick.
- The cornbread is ready when it forms a slightly tight crumb when poked. Enjoy!

Stuffed Zucchini Logs

Serving: 4 to 6 people

This dish is pretty simple and can be modified to your liking. I try to make it work with what's in season or with what looks best at the store. For adult portions, account for 2 halves per person. Try to buy large zucchinis or substitute with bell peppers, portobello caps, or acorn squash halves. Feel free to substitute where desired.

To make this recipe work, you must use a binder (cheeses & or egg) with a base filling of some sort (sautéed veggies, beans, a cooked grain, meat, or both). This can be converted to a vegetarian meal by omitting the meat and bumping up the protein (keeping the beans & even adding a complete protein like quinoa). No time to make the sauce; just use your favorite store brand. Get creative!

Tools Needed: a melon baller or a metal teaspoon, a sheet pan, a wooden spoon, a large sauté pan, a sauce pot, a large bowl & foil or parchment

Ingredients (Zucchini Logs & Filling)

- 4 large zucchinis (one per person)
- 1 lb ground turkey or pork-free sausage
- 2-4 tbsp fresh basil
- 2-3 cloves garlic (minced)
- 4 roma or plum tomatoes (diced)
- 16 oz ricotta cheese
- 1 cup frozen chopped spinach (defrosted & drained)
- 8 oz garbanzo beans (drained & rinsed)
- ¼ cup panko breadcrumbs
- 2 cups Italian cheese blend
- 2 tbsp fresh parsley (chopped)
- ½ onion (small diced)
- 1 egg (beaten)
- 2 tbsp olive oil (or as needed)

Spices (for the filling) – salt, pepper, Italian seasoning, paprika & granulated garlic to taste

Simple Marinara (optional):

- 2 ea 16 oz cans crushed tomato
- 4 oz tomato paste
- 33.5 oz of plain tomato sauce or purée
- 3 garlic cloves (minced)
- ¼ to ½ cup fruity white wine
- 1 tbsp fresh chopped basil (keep the stems)
- 1 tsp oregano (chopped)
- ½ onion (small diced)
- ½ carrot (peeled & whole)
- 2 to 3 tbsp sugar or agave nectar
- 1 tbsp olive oil

Spices- a pinch of pepper flakes, salt, pepper, Italian seasoning, onion powder & granulated garlic to taste

Prep & Procedure:
The Sauce

- Preheat the sauce pot on med-low heat.
- Add the olive oil & lightly sauté the onions, garlic & pepper flakes until aromatic and translucent.
- Add the tomato paste & spices. sauté for about a minute
- Deglaze the pot with about ¼ cup of wine. Add the remaining tomato products
- Add the carrot, whole basil stems with the herb attached, and 1 tbsp. of sweetener at a time (tt). Simmer on low for 15- 30 minutes, stirring occasionally.

Discard the basil stems & carrots before serving, set aside, or keep warm on a low flame until the dish is complete. Don't forget to taste & adjust the spices if needed.

Zucchini Log Prep

- Line your sheet pan with parchment & pre-heat the oven to 375° F.
- Cut all the zucchini logs in half lengthwise

- Carefully hollow out the centers of the zucchini using the melon baller tool. Leave about ½ inch brim around the diameter of the zucchini. Also, be careful not to break the bottom of the veggie bowl. Hold them while scooping the innards for more control. Chop up the innards to be included with the veggie mix (the filling).

The Filling

- Add 1 tbsp olive oil to the sauté pan, brown the meat & season it with the spices
- Once browned & cooked, remove the meat from the pan, drain off any excess fat & set it aside in a bowl.
- Add 1 tbsp olive oil to the same pan. Add the garlic, a pinch of pepper flakes, the zucchini innards & the onion. Sauté slightly until aromatic.
- Add the tomatoes. Cook for about 1 minute. Season lightly tt (season as we go to layer flavors)
- Add the veggie mixture to the bowl of meat. Add the spinach too.
- Deglaze the pan with a splash of wine or broth to scrape up the brown bits & add this to the bowl.
- Add half of the chopped basil & parsley. Reserve the rest to garnish the completed dish.

Finish The Log & Filling Prep

- Lightly season the hallowed zucchini with salt & pepper.
- Add the ricotta & chickpeas (garbanzo) to the bowl with the cooked mixture.
- Beat the egg in a small bowl & quickly mix it in after the ricotta is added. The cold cheese will drop the temperature of the mixture, which will help to avoid scrambling the egg.

Let's Stuff Em'

- Stuff the zucchini halves in a nice tight mound with the filling.
- In a smaller bowl, mix the shredded cheese with about 1 tbsp of the chopped herbs and about ¼ cup of panko.
- Sprinkle & press the cheesy topping on the top of each half. Drizzle with a little olive oil
- Bake for about 15 to 20 minutes in an oven preheated to 375°F. Or until they reach an internal temperature of 185°F.

Wait….

- Before serving the zucchini logs, re-taste the sauce
- Now's the time to tweak & adjust the seasonings accordingly. Check for a balance of sweet to the natural tang of the tomato. Add more sugar or sweetener of choice if needed.
- Add a bit of water or broth if it has gotten too thick. Finish your homemade marinara with some of the fresh chopped basil & oregano (remember to save a bit for garnishing). Add & stir thoroughly
- Once the sauce is perfect, plate the cheesy stuffed zucchini logs
- Serve them in a bed of hot marinara sauce & with optional garlic bread.
- Garnish with the remaining basil & parsley herb mix. Freshly shaved pecorino or parmesan would be a great final addition!

Chef's Tip: *If there's any excess filling, save it for the next day!* You could use it up in other ways… Here's an easy option: Create a fully loaded quiche. Add the extra filling to a prepared savory pie crust with a sprinkle of cheese. Simply whisk up about 6 to 8 eggs with ¼ cup of cream, season with s & p. Then pour the savory custard directly over the pie filling. Bake it in a preheated oven until the custard is set. Garnish & allow it to cool slightly before cutting. Voila, breakfast or lunch is complete!

Featuring Stuffed Zucchini Logs – This version excludes the ricotta, has navy beans & mixed cheeses

Sweet Potato Mash – Close Up

Sweet Potato Mash – Full View

Sweet Potato Mash

Yields: about 6 portions

Ingredients

3- 4 large, sweet potatoes

½ cup coconut milk

1 tbsp. butter

About ¼ cup brown sugar (to taste)

½-to 1 tbsp pure vanilla extract

A splash of heavy cream (about 2 tbsp. or as needed)

Water (as needed)

Tools Needed- veggie peeler, a large 4-6 qtr. pot, an electric beater or heavy-duty whisk, a wooden spoon, a colander or strainer & a can opener (for coconut milk)

Spices- season to taste with cinnamon, salt, white pepper & a pinch of cayenne

Method & Procedure

- Rinse & peel the sweet potatoes
- Cut them into large uniform chunks
- Boil the potatoes until they are fork-tender & ready for mashing
- Strain the tender potatoes in a sink & allow them to drain until dry
- Return the sweet potatoes back to the pot
- Using the hand mixer, beat them on high until fluffy & lump free
- Add the butter, spices to taste & the cream, and mix thoroughly using a wooden spoon
- Slowly add the coconut milk until the mash has reached your desired thickness
- Taste & adjust the spices & sweetness to your liking. Note: adding maple extract or maple syrup as half of the sweetener is also a scrumptious alternative
- This mash is a tasty treat by itself but can be complemented by candied pecans & a crack of black pepper. It will nicely accompany the brown sugar bourbon hens.

Whole Split Chicken

Whole Split Chicken with Parmesan Creamed Spinach

Yields: about 8 portions

This recipe is relatively easy to prepare. It is my version of a whole butterflied chicken. Don't underestimate its simplicity! Not only does the bird cook faster, but it showcases crispy skin on the exterior with moist, flavorful meat inside. My whole split chicken is definitely a simple delight! This recipe is in honor of my mother, Vivian, who taught me the key to roasting whole poultry— smearing butter & aromatics under the skin. Get creative & apply this same concept using different herbs & spices for other flavor combinations.

Tools Needed:

A sheet pan, kitchen shears, a micro-plane, chef's knife & cutting board, a baster or ladle spoon, a trash bowl, paper towels, a small bowl for the butter, a large skillet or high-sided pan & a cheese grater

The Chicken

Ingredients:

- 1 whole chicken (organic & without the innards)
- 6 garlic cloves
- extra virgin olive oil (as needed)
- About 4 tbsp. chopped herbs (parsley, rosemary, oregano & or thyme)
- 1 lemon (zest & juice)
- Spices (season to taste- I used about ½ tsp of each) smoked paprika, ground cumin, onion powder, crushed red pepper flakes (optional), black pepper, granulated garlic & sea salt

Prep the Chicken:

- Zest the lemon & save the zest for later. Juice the lemon, reserving 1 tbsps. of juice for the compound butter. Set the remaining juice aside. It will be used later to flavor the pan drippings.
- Wash & pat dry the herbs. Mince the garlic finely or into a paste.
- Create your spice mix by combining the above spices & adding salt to taste.
- Get a small bowl & add the softened butter, about 2 tbsp. EVOO, the spice mix (about 1 tbsp.), half of the garlic, the lemon zest & about 2 tbsp. of chopped herbs.
- Mix up the compound butter until combined & set it aside.

- Before handling the chicken, be sure to have about 8 large paper towel sheets torn off & waiting near the sink area.
- Prep the sink area first. Wash it thoroughly. Have the sheet pan, kitchen shears, trash bowl & paper towel sheets nearby.
- Place the whole chicken in a clean sink with the water on cold & in a slow stream.
- Have a trash bowl or bag nearby for easy access & to avoid dripping chicken germs.
- Remove the innards (if any) and discard them in the trash bowl.
- Flip the bird skin side down, being careful not to rip the skin on top.
- Using a sharp pair of kitchen shears, remove the backbone by cutting along each side. Also, discard any unwanted parts or gut fragments.
- Rinse away any debris & flip the chicken back over to skin side up.
- Now, pull off any remaining feathers, yellow skin, or excess fat.
- Once again, rinse away any debris. Place the chicken on a sheet pan, beginning with the flesh side up (open side).
- Lightly pat the flesh side dry with 4 of the paper towels.
- Spread about ¼ of the compound butter all over the flesh.
- Season the fleshy side of the butterflied chicken with a bit of the spice mix made earlier. Be sure to leave some for the top side.
- Flip the bird over to skin side up. Using your fingers, carefully separate the skin from the flesh. Do this all the way down to the tops of the thighs.
- Pat the skin dry using the remaining paper towels. This will help the compound butter to spread nicely.
- Now, add blobs of flavored butter underneath the skin. Press gently on top of the filled skin to push & smear the butter all around underneath the skin. Repeat this process on both the left & right sides of the bird until the entire chicken has been done.
- Finally, rub the top of the chicken skin with some of the butter mix. Season it all around using the spice blend.

Cook the Chicken:

- Time to bake! Place the seasoned butter-rubbed chicken into a 375°F preheated oven. Add about 1 cup of liquid to a corner of the sheet pan along with the lemon juice. This will keep the chicken moist while the skin side crisps.
- Begin basting the bird after 30 minutes of baking. Then, baste it about every 15 minutes or so. You may have to add a bit more broth or water to the pan here & there.
- You will be surprised at how quickly a butterflied chicken can cook! Depending on your oven, it usually takes about 1 ½ hours. As the chicken has been split, this promotes a shorter & more even cooking time.
- Note: As the chicken roasts, it's time to tidy up, clean/ sanitize the prep area, and create the side.

The Parmesan Creamed Spinach

Ingredients:

- 3 ea. 12 oz. bags frozen chopped spinach or about 2 ½ ea. 16oz bags of fresh
- The remaining minced garlic (3 cloves)
- extra virgin olive oil (as needed)
- ½ to 1 cup grated parmesan
- 1 ½ cups heavy cream
- ½ cup veggie broth
- Spices (season to taste): smoked paprika, ground cumin, onion powder, crushed red pepper flakes (optional), black pepper, granulated garlic & sea salt

Prep & cook the Spinach

- Before starting, remember to thoroughly wash your hands, and clean/ sanitize the sinks & all affected areas where the chicken was prepped.
- Keep in mind that this is a relatively quick side dish. It may only take about 10 minutes from start to finish. So, I recommend cooking this when the chicken is almost done.
- Preheat a large skillet or pan to medium heat. Add a drizzle of EVOO.

- Add a ½ tsp of crushed red pepper flakes & the garlic. Stir it & immediately begin adding the spinach to wilt down. Stir frequently & season to taste. Continue this process until all the spinach has been added to the pan. Use this strategy for fresh spinach.
- If using frozen, simply add all the frozen spinach to the pan after lightly browning the garlic. It will take a few minutes longer to cook as it must first thaw.
- Add the cream, broth & parmesan into the pan. Start by adding about ½ cup of parmesan. It may take a bit more to get that mildly sweet & nutty parmesan taste. The above steps can be done even if the frozen spinach is used & hasn't yet thawed. Stir it around
- Taste & adjust the spice levels of the spinach. Season it to taste as you choose or with the spices mentioned. When seasoning, be mindful that the parmesan is a bit salty. I would wait to add the salt afterward.
- Turn off the heat once it has thickened & is still a vibrant green. Don't cook the life out of your veggies!
- All done! It's ready to serve alongside the whole split chicken. You can even lightly brown a few sliced cloves of garlic for an intensified garlicky finish.
- Remember to allow the chicken to rest for at least 3 to 5 minutes before carving to retain juices. It pairs beautifully with the saucy creamed spinach.

Chef's Tip: This meal would be another great option to have to go into the Sabbath on Friday night! *You could simply prep the chicken ahead of time. Or, even assemble it a day or two prior as an oven ready meal. Just throw it into the oven while doing chores Friday afternoon, cook the side when it's nearly done & relax. Bon appetite!*

Chapter 13: Unleavened Bread

- Basic Vanilla
- Blackberry Streusel
- Lemon Cheesecake
- Raspberry Coffee Cake

Something to Think About…

Are eggs a leavening agent? Let me break it down. Eggs are technically a form of protein. Yet, they can be manipulated in many ways. They can emulsify or bring two unlike ingredients together (like oil & water). They implement moisture & texture to baked goods.

Finally, if aerated, eggs can definitely become a leavening agent. So, be mindful not to aerate the eggs while preparing unleavened bread recipes. Unlike unleavened flatbreads, the following bakes are more similar to brownies or dense cakes. Remember not to incorporate any additives that contain leavening agents (like cookie pieces). Be sure to follow the upcoming instructions carefully to avoid developing air while preparing these recipes!

Tips for Success:

*Use the correct mixing tool: Use the paddle attachment for mixing bowls or a strong wooden spoon. Never use a whisk!

*Use the creaming mixing method while combining ingredients: Cream the butter & sugar together first. Now, combine all the dry ingredients. Then separately combine all wet ingredients. Finally, bring it all together by alternating & blending in the two (into the creamed butter & sugar mix).

*Measure & Scrape: For accuracy, use the correct tool & remember to level it out by scraping! While measuring, be sure to use the correct measuring utensils. If measuring a dry ingredient, use dry measuring cups and vice versa when using liquid. This should be done as they both vary slightly in volume. Also, be mindful to level out your dry measurements. This may make all the difference. Scoop a mounding cup, tap it to remove air pockets & finally scrape the top level using a flat edge. Sifting dry ingredients or whisking out any lumps isn't required but it is certainly another vital tip for success.

Use Parchment Paper: This extra step is not necessary, but it could offer a bit of flexibility. Not only does it prevent sticking, but it also does a bit more. Parchment can aid in speedy removal should you nearly overbake the UB. Getting it out of the heat conductor (hot pan) can definitely help the UB to cool faster & reduce carryover cooking!

Biblical References to Unleavened Bread

(23) For I have received of the Lord that which also I delivered unto you, That the Lord Jesus the same night in which he was betrayed took bread:

(24) And when he had given thanks, he break it, and said, Take, eat: this is my body, which is broken for you: this do in remembrance of me.

(25) After the same manner also he took the cup, when he had supped, saying, This cup is the new testament in my blood: this do ye, as oft as ye drink it, in remembrance of me.

(26) For as often as ye eat this bread, and drink this cup, ye do shew the Lord's death till he come.

(27) Wherefore whosoever shall eat this bread, and drink this cup of the Lord unworthily, shall be guilty of the body and blood of the Lord.

(28) But let a man examine himself, and so let him eat of that bread, and drink of that cup.

(29) For he that eateth and drinketh unworthily, eateth and drinketh damnation to himself, not discerning the Lord's body.

(30) For this cause many are weak and sickly among you, and many sleep.

1 Corinthians 11:23-30

Keep the Feast of Unleavened Bread

(Passover)

Thou shalt keep the feast of unleavened bread: (thou shalt eat unleavened bread seven days, as I commanded thee, in the time appointed of the month Abib; for in it thou camest out from Egypt: and none shall appear before me empty:)

Exodus 23:15

[15] Seven days shall ye eat unleavened bread; even the first day ye shall put away leaven out of your houses: for whosoever eateth leavened bread from the first day until the seventh day, that soul shall be cut off from Israel.

[16] And in the first day there shall be an holy convocation, and in the seventh day there shall be an holy convocation to you; no manner of work shall be done in them, save that which every man must eat, that only may be done of you.

[17] And ye shall observe the feast of unleavened bread; for in this selfsame day have I brought your armies out of the land of Egypt: therefore shall ye observe this day in your generations by an ordinance for ever.

[18] In the first month, on the fourteenth day of the month at even, ye shall eat unleavened bread, until the one and twentieth day of the month at even.

[19] Seven days shall there be no leaven found in your houses: for whosoever eateth that which is leavened, even that soul shall be cut off from the congregation of Israel, whether he be a stranger, or born in the land.

[20] Ye shall eat nothing leavened; in all your habitations shall ye eat unleavened bread.

Exodus 12:15-20

[6] Your glorying is not good. Know ye not that a little leaven leaveneth the whole lump?

[7] Purge out therefore the old leaven, that ye may be a new lump, as ye are unleavened. For even Christ our passover is sacrificed for us:

[8] Therefore let us keep the feast, not with old leaven, neither with the leaven of malice and wickedness; but with the unleavened bread of sincerity and truth.

1 Corinthians 5:6-8

The Possibilities Are Endless...
Here are a few U. B. pictures for inspiration

Blueberry Cheese Danish

Gooey Candy Bar

Upside Down Caramel Apple

Chocolate Swirl

White Chocolate Mocha

Banana Foster UB Muffins – featured on a cold Sabbath brunch platter

Chocolate Chip Cookie

Inverted Key Lime Pie UB from start to finish – Featuring a lime infused batter with a tart citrus cream filling & topped with a zesty lime glaze

Inverted Key Lime Pie Batter

Baked & awaiting glaze

Lightly glazed IKLP UB... more is needed for a finishing touch

Inverted Key Lime Pie UB (fully glazed & complete)

Pumpkin Cream UB

(a fusion of pumpkin pie & cheesecake)

Basic Vanilla UB

The Basic U.B.

Yields: 1 pan

This delicious sweet unleavened bread is not something to eat every day. This recipe is a basic blend that can be manipulated into different flavor combinations. I recommend that you play around with the basic batter first. Then, you will know what to expect from a good texture & consistency. Nearly any brownie or cake recipe can be transformed into unleavened bread by removing the leavening components.

Ingredients (The Basic UB)

- 2 sticks unsalted butter (room temperature, soft or melted)
- 1 tbsp extract flavoring of choice (I used vanilla)
- 2 cups of sugar
- 2 cups AP flour
- A pinch of sea salt
- 3 whole eggs
- A slash of milk (about ¼ cup)

Tools Needed:

A standing or electric mixer, a large bowl, a liquid measuring cup, a rubber spatula, a fork, measuring spoons, dry measuring cups, a 13" x 9" rectangular cake pan, a bowl/ rubber spatula or spoon

Chef's Tip- Remember, good quality ingredients form great quality results! I recommend that you use pure extracts whenever possible & good quality ingredients. Remember that this is unleavened bread. Be sure to avoid excess aeration. Do not use the whisk. You should use the paddle attachment. If making this recipe by hand, combine the ingredients using a wooden spoon.

Eat this treat in moderation. Serve it in small squares or eat it warm with your favorite complementary ice cream.

Prep the Ingredients

- Melt the butter.
- Using a standing or electric hand mixer, cream the melted butter & sugar until somewhat fluffy & pale. If you prefer a more cake-like result, use softened butter instead of melted.
- While the butter is creaming, let's prep the other ingredients.
- Sift the flour & salt or any added dry ingredients (like cocoa powder).
- Crack the room-temperature eggs in a separate container & add in the flavoring extract (vanilla, almond, raspberry, etc.). Stir in a splash of milk. Start with about 1/8 cup. More will be added at the end if it's needed. Mix it with a fork & set aside.
- Return to the creaming butter & sugar.
- Turn off the mixer & scrape down the sides of the bowl.

Let's Mix It Up

- Begin alternating the dry & liquid ingredients to blend into the creamed butter & sugar mix. You will likely do this using about 1/3 of the dry ingredients or liquid ingredients at one time. Continue alternating the dry with the wet (egg mixture) until all the items are incorporated.
- Be sure to scrape down the mixing bowl between the additions.
- The batter should resemble a slightly thinner brownie batter.
- Add about another 1/8 cup of milk if needed. The dairy can be substituted with your milk of choice (almond, 2%, half n half, coconut, or even cream). Be mindful that certain milks may alter the final texture of the unleavened bread. You may want to attempt this recipe with traditional milk before experimenting. For fluffier UB, try adding an oz of cream cheese during the sugar & butter creaming phase. You could even use a tbsp or so of mayo or sour cream for similar results.
- I like to taste a tiny bit of the batter to ensure that there's enough flavor. If it's lacking, adjust it by adding a splash of more extract.

Time to Bake

- Bake this brownie-like unleavened bread in a 325°F pre-heated oven. The cook time may vary depending on your oven.
- Lightly sprinkle a fine dusting of sugar over the top before baking for that professional crispy top.
- Bake for 45 minutes to an hour or until it is crusty on top & forms a tight crumb when a toothpick is inserted in the center. As this treat is dense, I often take a small plug out of the middle using a paring knife to ensure doneness. Enjoy!

Blackberry Streusel UB

Blackberry Streusel U.B.

Yields: 1 pan

This treat begins with the basic unleavened bread recipe. It is topped & baked with a gooey blackberry blend & finished with streusel crumbles. You can even make other variations by simply swapping out the type of berries. Play with it & make it your own! Remember to store any leftovers in an airtight container & eat within 2-3 days.

Tools Needed:

A standing or electric mixer, a large bowl, liquid measuring cup, dry measuring cups, rubber spatulas, a fork, measuring spoons, a 13" x 9" rectangular cake pan, a fine zester or micro-plane, 2 bowls & a spoon

Chef's Tip- Be sure that the eggs & butter are at room temperature. This will allow them to incorporate better during production & even promote a more tender cake.

Ingredients: (Basic U.B. Batter)

See the basic unleavened bread recipe.

Follow the instructions to create the basic unleavened bread recipe. For a more lemon-enhanced flavor, substitute most of the milk in the basic recipe for fresh or bottled lemon juice. Then pour the batter into a buttered rectangular cake pan. This UB is similar to a poke cake except it is cooked partially before poking. Just bake it in a 325°F pre-heated oven until half done. Remove it from the oven & set this aside until the berry topping is ready to layer on top.

Let's get started!

The Blackberry Topping (Ingredients)

- 6-8 oz fresh blackberries
- 1 tsp corn starch
- 1 jar seedless blackberry jam (10 oz jar)
- 1 lemon (zest & juice)
- Use half the zest in the batter, save half for the berry mix
- 3 tbsp water
- 1 tbsp vanilla extract

- 1 tbsp lemon juice (measure from the juiced & zested lemon)
- About ¼ cup raw sugar

Prep the Berry Mix

- Pour the jar of seedless blackberry jam into a medium-sized bowl.
- Dilute the jam with the water & lemon juice, then mix it together until smooth.
- Rinse the fresh blackberries & pat them dry. Slice them into thirds or halves to form cylinders.
- Lightly coat them in the cornstarch.
- Gently mix the fresh berries into the jam mixture. Set aside.

The Streusel Topping (Ingredients)

- ½ stick diced cold butter
- ½-1 cup AP flour
- ¼ cup sliced almonds (optional)
- ½ cup raw sugar
- ½ tsp lemon zest
- ½ tsp vanilla extract

Prep the Streusel Topping Mix

- Cut the cold butter into small cubes & put it into a bowl
- Add the flour & other ingredients
- Cut the flour mixture into the butter using a fork
- The mix should begin to look grainy
- If it does not hold to form a crumbly ball when squeezing a little together, add more butter
- If it is too gummy or pasty, add more flour until it will form small pea-like pieces & hold its shape into a ball when squeezed.
- Chill the streusel until it is needed.

Assembly: Let's Put Them Together

- Return to the half-baked unleavened bread. Delicately poke holes all around using a fork or butter knife. Dollop the berry jam concoction all over the top, covering the entire surface area of the cake. Carefully spread it evenly
- Remove the streusel topping from the fridge. Crumble it in different-sized clumps all over the top of the UB.
- Finally, sprinkle the top of the whole UB mix with a fine dusting of raw sugar. You can add a pinch of cinnamon & any remaining lemon zest to this sugar dusting.

Time to Bake

- Bake this heavenly treat in a 325°F pre-heated oven. The cook time may vary depending on your oven.
- Bake for another 35 minutes or so. To test for doneness, remove a small plug. Be sure to use a paring knife to poke through the berry layer down to the regular cake. Do this at the center. When removed, the knife should show signs of a tight cake crumb following the gooey berry topping.

Let's Finish It

- If the crumble topping has not browned thoroughly once the cake is fully baked, no need to worry!
- Finish it in the broiler for about 30 seconds or until the streusel is lightly golden & crisp. DON'T STEP AWAY DURING THIS PROCESS! I've made this mistake before & accidentally over browned the topping.
- Remember to store leftovers in an air-tight container once fully cooled to preserve freshness & shelf life. Enjoy!

Cheesecake UB

Unbaked Cheesecake UB

Lemon Cheesecake U.B.

Yields: 1 pan

This treat begins with the basic unleavened bread recipe. It is topped & baked with a lemon cheesecake mix. You can even make other variations by simply swapping out the type of citrus. As always, have fun & don't be afraid to explore; make it your way! Remember to store any leftovers in the fridge after cooling. It is indeed a form of cheesecake & quite perishable.

Ingredients: See the basic unleavened bread recipe.

Ingredients (The Cheesecake Batter)

- 1 egg
- 8 oz cream cheese
- 4 oz sour cream
- 1 lemon (zest & juice)
- Use half the zest in the batter, save half for the end
- 1 tbsp AP flour
- 1 tsp vanilla, ¼ tsp lemon extract
- 2 tbsp lemon juice
- ¼ cup raw sugar

Tools Needed:

A standing or electric mixer, a large bowl, liquid measuring cup, dry measuring cups, a rubber spatula, a fork, measuring spoons, a 13" x 9" rectangular cake pan, a fine zester or micro-plane, a bowl/ rubber spatula or spoon & an offset cake spatula

Chef's Tip- Be sure that the egg, cream cheese & butter are at room temperature. This will allow them to incorporate better during production & even promote a more tender cake.

Follow the instructions to create the basic unleavened bread recipe. For a more lemon-enhanced flavor, substitute most of the milk in the basic recipe for fresh or bottled lemon juice. Then fill a buttered rectangular cake pan with two-thirds of that batter. You can make a personal pan with the remaining third. Don't bake it yet! Set this aside until the cheesecake batter is ready for assembly.

Prep the Cheesecake Batter

- Using a standing or electric hand mixer, beat the cream cheese & sugar together until creamy.
- Add the flour & incorporate it starting on low speed.
- Stop & scrape down the sides & bottom of the mixing bowl.
- Thoroughly mix in the remaining ingredients. Remember to scrape down the sides & mix the batter again briefly.
- I like to taste a tiny bit of the batter to ensure that there's enough flavor. If it's lacking, adjust it by adding a splash more of vanilla & or lemon juice. A pinch of salt may very well do the trick!

Let's Put Them Together

- Return to the pre-assembled basic unleavened bread.
- Pour the cheesecake batter directly over the top of the pan of lemon flavored basic unleavened.
- Using an offset or rubber spatula, evenly spread the cheesecake batter directly over the top of the basic UB.
- Knock out the extra air bubbles by gently lifting & tapping the pan down on a level surface. Be careful not to tilt or lift the pan of batter in a way that would make the cake uneven.

Time to Bake

- Bake this delectable treat in a 325°F pre-heated oven. The cook time may vary depending on your oven.
- Bake for 45 minutes to an hour. It may even take a bit longer. To test it, use a paring knife to poke through the cheesecake layer down to the regular cake. Do this at the center. When removed, the knife should show signs of a tight cake crumb residue. I often sacrifice a small portion in the middle to ensure that the cake is fully cooked. The cheesecake part should be set & have a tight jiggle. It should not wiggle. Once both the cheesecake is set & the cake forms a tight crumb, the unleavened cheesecake bread is ready!

Let's Finish It

- Allow it to sit & cool down to room temperature before storing. Avoid too much movement or rapid cooling in the freezer as it may cause the cake to crack. If it does, no biggie. It will still taste delicious!

- Once cooled, garnish the top of the cheesecake UB with the remaining lemon zest.
- Remember to store it covered in the fridge to preserve freshness & shelf life. Enjoy!

Raspberry Coffee Cake UB

Raspberry Coffee Cake UB – Close Up

Raspberry Coffee Cake U.B.

Yields: 1 pan

Start with the basic unleavened bread recipe and transform it into a new variation. Have fun & get those creative thoughts going; the possibilities are endless!

Ingredients (Begin with the Basic UB Mix)

- 2 sticks unsalted butter (room temperature, soft)
- 1 tbsp vanilla extract
- 2 cups of sugar
- 2 cups AP flour
- A pinch of sea salt
- 3 whole eggs
- A slash of dairy (about ¼ cup)

The Additives: 1 cup frozen raspberries, zest of 1 lemon, 1 tbsp lemon juice, a few fresh raspberries to garnish

The Sauce (Raspberry Coulis): 1 cup frozen raspberries, ½ to 1 cup water, 1 tbsp lemon juice and sugar to taste. Add all ingredients into a blender & purée until smooth. Strain to remove the seeds. Taste, adjust and even thicken with a little cornstarch slurry if desired. *Note that it must be heated to a simmer to thicken with a cornstarch slurry.*

The Topping (Streusel): ½ to 1 cup AP flour, a pinch of salt, ¼ cup brown sugar, ¼ cup raw sugar, some of the lemon zest and a ½ stick of butter

Tools Needed:

A standing or electric mixer, a large bowl, liquid measuring cup, dry measuring cups, a rubber spatula, a fork, measuring spoons, a blender (for the sauce), a fine strainer, a 13" x 9" rectangular cake pan, a bowl/ jar with lid & a rubber spatula or spoon

Tip- Remove the eggs from the fridge 1-2 hours ahead. Room temperature eggs will incorporate into the batter better. *Should you forget to bring your eggs to room temp:* Simply add the cold eggs to a bowl filled with hot tap water. Let them sit for at least 15 minutes before use. The eggs will quickly reach the desired temperature in a fraction of the time! Remember that this is unleavened bread. Be sure to avoid excess aeration. Do not use the whisk. You should use the paddle attachment. If making this recipe by hand, combine the ingredients using a wooden spoon.

Getting Started

- Begin with the streusel topping, combine all its ingredients & use a fork to mix it until it forms pea-like crumbs.
- Test it out, the topping should hold together when squeezed.
- Allow it to chill in the fridge while you assemble the batter.
- Preheat your oven to 325°F.

Prep the Ingredients

- Melt the butter.
- Using a standing mixer, cream the melted butter & sugar until somewhat pale. If you prefer a more cake-like result, use softened butter instead of melted.
- While the butter is creaming, let's prep the other ingredients.
- Sift the flour & salt together and stir.
- Reserve 1 tbsp of the dry mix for later.
- Crack the room temperature eggs in a separate container & add in the vanilla extract.
- Stir in a splash of milk. Start with about 1/8 cup. More will be added at the end if its needed. Mix it with a fork & set aside.
- Let's return to the creamed butter & sugar.
- Turn off the mixer & scrape down the sides of the bowl.

Let's Mix It Up

- Begin alternating the dry & liquid ingredients to blend into the creamed butter & sugar mix. You will likely do this using about 1/3 of the dry ingredients or liquid ingredients at one time. Continue alternating the dry with the wet (egg mixture) until all the items are incorporated.
- Be sure to scrape down the mixing bowl between the additions.
- The batter should resemble a slightly thinner brownie batter.

- Add about another 1/8 cup of milk if needed. The dairy can be substituted with your milk of choice (I used half n half).
- I like to taste a tiny bit of the batter to ensure that there's enough flavor. If it's lacking, adjust it by adding a splash more extract or lemon. You could even add a bit of raspberry flavoring…
- Sprinkle the reserved dry mix over 1 cup of frozen raspberries. Gently coat them in the flour until lightly dusted. Do this as the berries are frozen.
- Carefully fold the dusted frozen raspberries into the batter. They will make it slightly thicker because of the coldness.
- Add the batter to a parchment-lined cake pan. The parchment will make it easy to remove from the pan later.
- Try to spread the batter as best as you can without breaking up the berries. This will take a bit of finesse; a light delicate hand.

Time to Bake

- Sprinkle the top of the bread with a few more raspberries (optional) & top with the streusel before baking.
- Bake the unleavened bread in a 325°F pre-heated oven. The cook time may vary depending on your oven.
- Lightly sprinkle a fine dusting of sugar over the top before baking to help promote browning.

Bake for 45 minutes to an hour or until it is crusty on top & forms a tight crumb when a toothpick is inserted in the center. Enjoy!

For in depth tips, watch my "how to make sweet unleavened bread" video on YouTube (Love in the Pot).

Helpful Charts

Smoking Points of Cooking Fats & Oils

Fat/Oil	Smoke Point °F	Smoke Point °C
Avocado Oil	570°F	271°C
Butter	250-200°F	120-150°C
Canola Oil (refined)	400°F	204°C
Coconut Oil (extra virgin)	350°F	177°C
Coconut Oil (refined)	450°F	232°C
Corn Oil	440°F	227°C
Flax seed Oil	225°F	107°C
Clarified Butter	485°F	252°C
Olive Oil (extra virgin)	375°F	191°C
Olive Oil (virgin)	391°F	199°C
Olive Oil (extra light)	468°F	242°C
Peanut Oil	450°F	232°C
Sesame Oil (unrefined)	350°F	177°C
Soybean Oil (refined)	460°F	238°C
Vegetable Shortening	360°F	182°C

A Rainbow of Health
What the different colors of fruits and veggies mean to you

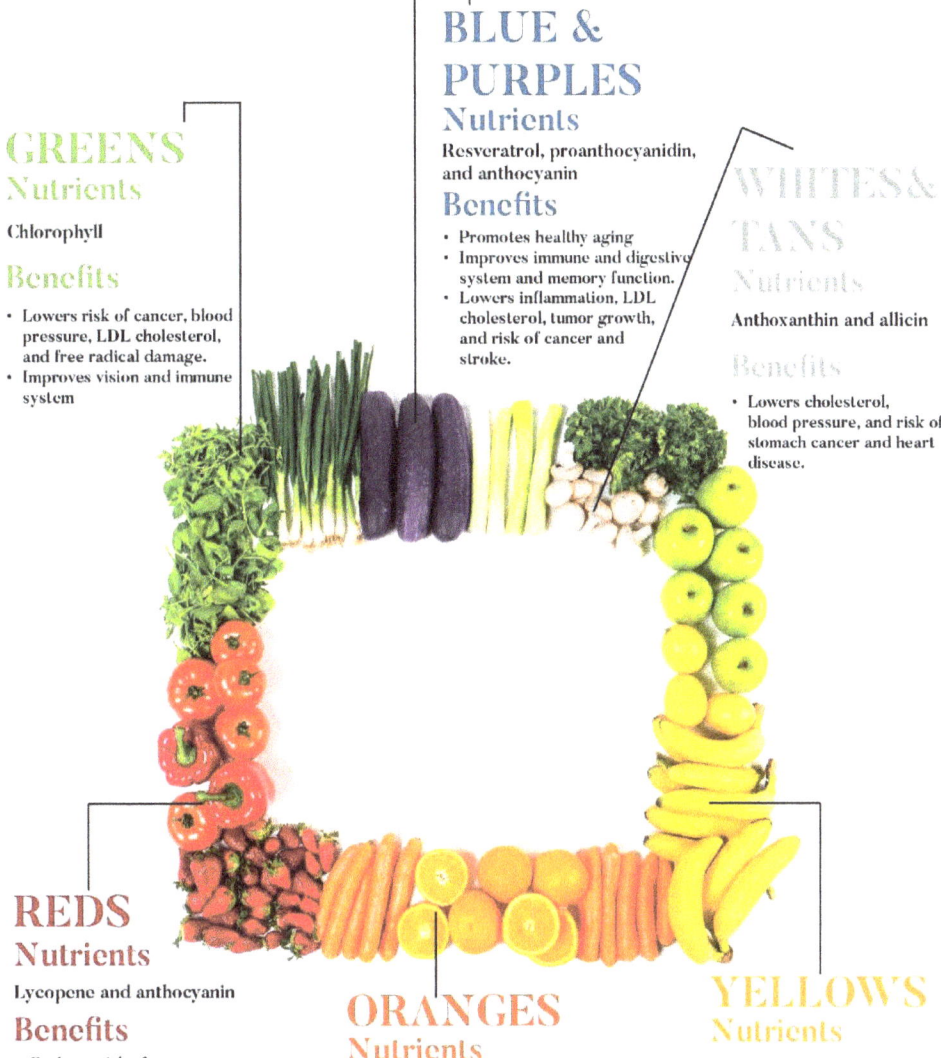

GREENS
Nutrients

Chlorophyll

Benefits
- Lowers risk of cancer, blood pressure, LDL cholesterol, and free radical damage.
- Improves vision and immune system

BLUE & PURPLES
Nutrients

Resveratrol, proanthocyanidin, and anthocyanin

Benefits
- Promotes healthy aging
- Improves immune and digestive system and memory function.
- Lowers inflammation, LDL cholesterol, tumor growth, and risk of cancer and stroke.

WHITES & TANS
Nutrients

Anthoxanthin and allicin

Benefits
- Lowers cholesterol, blood pressure, and risk of stomach cancer and heart disease.

REDS
Nutrients

Lycopene and anthocyanin

Benefits
- Reduces risk of cancer
- Lowers blood pressure and LDL cholesterol levels.
- Helps maintain memory function, urinary track health.
- Fights off infections and supports joint tissue.

ORANGES
Nutrients

Carotenoids and citrus bioflavonoids

Benefits
- Improves brain functions and decreases muscle cramps
- Lowers risk of cancer and heart disease
- Increases efficiency of the immune system

YELLOWS
Nutrients

Lutein and zeaxanthin

Benefits
- Decreases risk of macular degeneration, and protect eyes from damage.
- Increases energy levels and immune system

Eating an assortment of colorful fruits and veggies provide your body with a wide range of vitamins, minerals, and nutrients. To get the most of these health benefits, it's recommended that you eat one serving from each color group every day.

How Long Does Food Last?

Here's what to **keep**...
and what to **toss**

	Freezer		Pantry		Fridge	
LUNCH MEAT	1-2 months	BREAD	5-7 days	BREAD	2 days	FRUIT
FISH	2-6 months	PEANUT BUTTER	6 months		3-4 days	BREAD DOUGH
GROUND MEAT	3-4 months	CEREAL	1 year		4 days	LEFTOVERS
BEEF-STEAK	6-12 months	RICE	1 year		3 months	BUTTER
WHOLE POULTRY	1 year	CANNED GOODS	1 year		1-2 weeks	CHEESE
BREAD	1 year	SALAD DRESSING	1 year		1-2 days	POULTRY
FRESH VEGGIES	1 year	JAM/SYRUP	1 year		3-5 days	STEAK
Fresh Fruit	1 year	PASTA	2 year		3-5 weeks	EGGS

Put this on your fridge as a reminder and guide.

If you are What you Eat, What **Color** are You?

You may have heard that eating 5-9 servings of vegetables and fruits each day is good for you. But did you know that eating a variety of COLORFUL foods is just as improtant? Use this chart to help you learn about the different FOOD COLOR GROUP, what nutrients they contain, and their health benefits. Check the boxes below when you have tried each item from the RAINBOW!

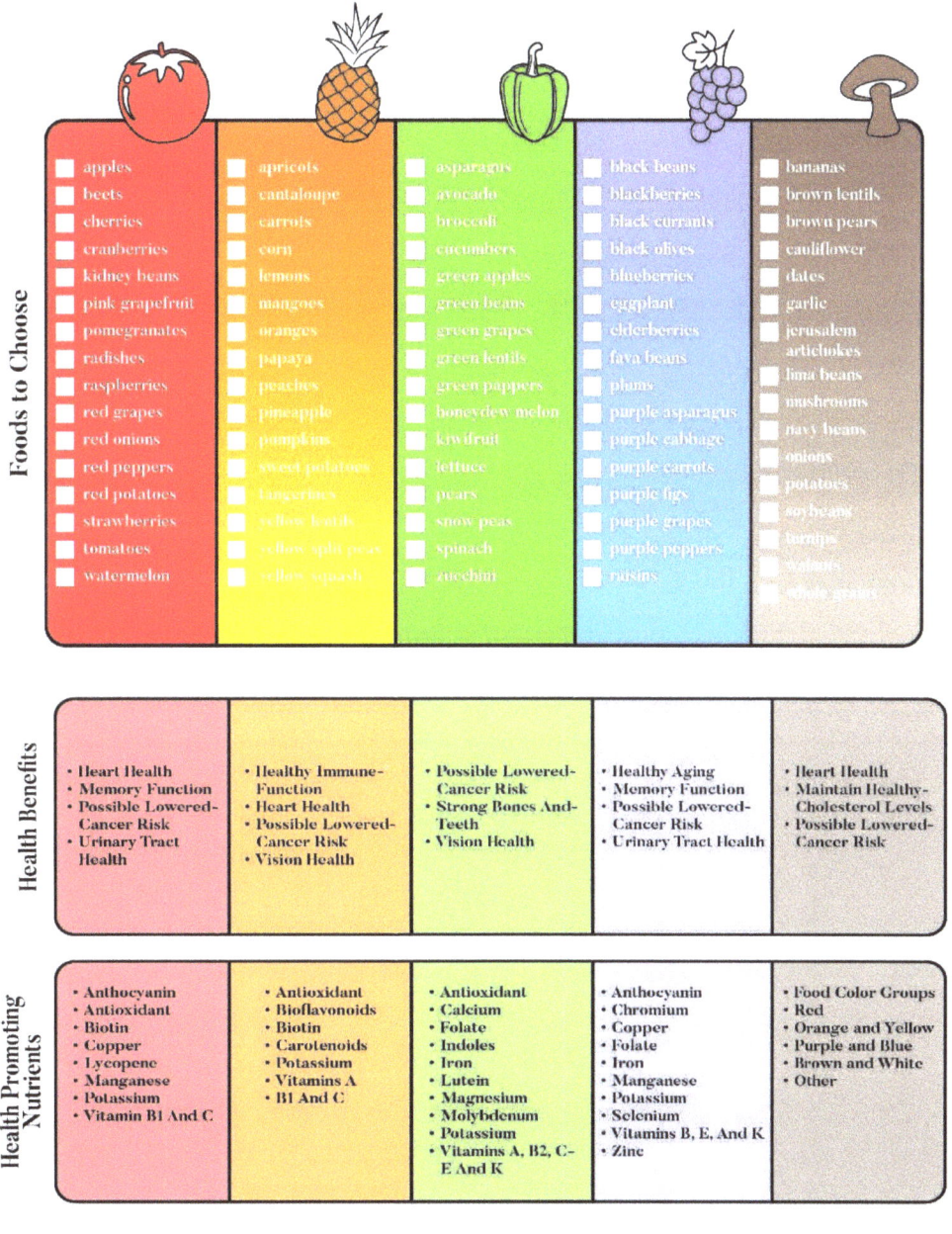

Foods to Choose

Red	Orange/Yellow	Green	Purple/Blue	Brown/White
☐ apples	☐ apricots	☐ asparagus	☐ black beans	☐ bananas
☐ beets	☐ cantaloupe	☐ avocado	☐ blackberries	☐ brown lentils
☐ cherries	☐ carrots	☐ broccoli	☐ black currants	☐ brown pears
☐ cranberries	☐ corn	☐ cucumbers	☐ black olives	☐ cauliflower
☐ kidney beans	☐ lemons	☐ green apples	☐ blueberries	☐ dates
☐ pink grapefruit	☐ mangoes	☐ green beans	☐ eggplant	☐ garlic
☐ pomegranates	☐ oranges	☐ green grapes	☐ elderberries	☐ jerusalem artichokes
☐ radishes	☐ papaya	☐ green lentils	☐ fava beans	☐ lima beans
☐ raspberries	☐ peaches	☐ green peppers	☐ plums	☐ mushrooms
☐ red grapes	☐ pineapple	☐ honeydew melon	☐ purple asparagus	☐ navy beans
☐ red onions	☐ pumpkins	☐ kiwifruit	☐ purple cabbage	☐ onions
☐ red peppers	☐ sweet potatoes	☐ lettuce	☐ purple carrots	☐ potatoes
☐ red potatoes	☐ tangerines	☐ pears	☐ purple figs	☐ soybeans
☐ strawberries	☐ yellow lentils	☐ snow peas	☐ purple grapes	☐ turnips
☐ tomatoes	☐ yellow split peas	☐ spinach	☐ purple peppers	☐ walnuts
☐ watermelon	☐ yellow squash	☐ zucchini	☐ raisins	☐ whole grains

Health Benefits

Red	Orange/Yellow	Green	Purple/Blue	Brown/White
• Heart Health • Memory Function • Possible Lowered-Cancer Risk • Urinary Tract Health	• Healthy Immune-Function • Heart Health • Possible Lowered-Cancer Risk • Vision Health	• Possible Lowered-Cancer Risk • Strong Bones And-Teeth • Vision Health	• Healthy Aging • Memory Function • Possible Lowered-Cancer Risk • Urinary Tract Health	• Heart Health • Maintain Healthy-Cholesterol Levels • Possible Lowered-Cancer Risk

Health Promoting Nutrients

Red	Orange/Yellow	Green	Purple/Blue	Brown/White
• Anthocyanin • Antioxidant • Biotin • Copper • Lycopene • Manganese • Potassium • Vitamin B1 And C	• Antioxidant • Bioflavonoids • Biotin • Carotenoids • Potassium • Vitamins A • B1 And C	• Antioxidant • Calcium • Folate • Indoles • Iron • Lutein • Magnesium • Molybdenum • Potassium • Vitamins A, B2, C-E And K	• Anthocyanin • Chromium • Copper • Folate • Iron • Manganese • Potassium • Selenium • Vitamins B, E, And K • Zinc	• Food Color Groups • Red • Orange and Yellow • Purple and Blue • Brown and White • Other

References

1. The Holy Bible With The Apocrypha

King James Version

Cambridge University Press

2. On Cooking, a textbook of culinary fundamentals

By Sarah R. Labensky & Alan M. Hause

3. ServSafe Coursebook (2001 FDA Food Code) Second Edition

National Restaurant Association (Education Foundation)

4. ServSafe Essentials (2009 FDA Food Code)

Fifth Edition National Restaurant Association

5. https://www.medicalnewstoday.com/articles/248958#_noHeaderPrefixedContent
6. https://chwbonline.com/top-10-health-benefits-lean-protein/
7. https://www.webmd.com/food-recipes/health-benefits-legumes
8. https://www.webmd.com/cancer/ss/slideshow-cancer-fighting-foods#:~:text=Dark%20green%20leafy%20vegetables%20such,lung%2C%20skin%2C%20and%20stomach.
9. https://parenting.firstcry.com/articles/magazine-10-surprising-dry-fruit-benefits/
10. https://www.helpguide.org/articles/healthy-eating/choosing-healthy-fats.htm
11. https://www.masterclass.com/articles/cooking-oils-and-smoke-points-what-to-know-and-how-to-choose

In loving memory of my mother, Vivian L. B. Holt, who taught me the basis to southern classics. As many of us have encountered, she experienced ups and downs in life. Despite it all, Vivian began a journey of self-renewal in her later years ("a just man falleth seven times & riseth up again", Proverbs 24:16).

To the best of her ability, she tried to keep God's commandments and to reform her life according to God's instructions (Romans 12:1-2). Knowing this, I'm hopeful that God will have mercy & reward her charitable efforts!

Bitter Sweet

By: Chana Israel

Sweet to see you at rest and without pain,

Bitter to see you and not be with you.

Thoughts of moments together,

Prevailing even through pain.

Prevailing through fire & turmoil,

Emerging from darkness into light again.

Looming from past sins,

Polishing the spirit within.

Through experience came beauty.

A new path of growth

Now at peace, mending what was once broken.

You prevailed through hard times,

Emerging from turmoil to bloom.

Kindness, charity, spunky joy and love,

All which embodied you.

How bitter sweet,

Bitter sweet to lose you!

www.ingramcontent.com/pod-product-compliance
Lightning Source LLC
Chambersburg PA
CBHW051310110526
44590CB00031B/4363